# faïthful

**100 DEVOTIONS INSPIRED BY CATS**

# purrs

# faithful purrs

## 100 DEVOTIONS INSPIRED BY CATS

**Editors of *All God's Creatures***

## *A Gift from Guideposts*

Thank you for your purchase! We want to express our gratitude for your support with a special gift just for you.

Dive into ***Spirit Lifters***, a complimentary e-book that will fortify your faith, offering solace during challenging moments. Its 31 carefully selected scripture verses will soothe and uplift your soul.

Please use the QR code or go to **guideposts.org/spiritlifters** to download.

**Faithful Purrs: 100 Devotions Inspired by Cats**

Published by Guideposts
100 Reserve Road, Suite E200
Danbury, CT 06810
Guideposts.org

Copyright © 2025 by Guideposts. All rights reserved.

This book, or parts thereof, may not be reproduced, stored in a retrieval system, or transmitted in any form or by any means, electronic, mechanical, photocopying, recording, or otherwise, without the written permission of the publisher.

Cover and interior design by Beth Meyer

Cover photo by MilanEXPO / Getty Images. Interior images: p. 22, 101cats; p. 23, danielwilliams; p. 44-45, 101cats; p. 64, Stephanie Stafford; p. 65, danielwilliams; p. 86, Sergeeva; p. 87, brunorbs; p. 108, rio Agusta; p. 109, danielwilliams; p. 130, Berk Ucak; p. 131, Nemika_Polted; p. 152, martinedoucet; p. 153, danielwilliams; p. 174, Gabriele Grassi; p. 175, ynoclub; p. 196, Andyworks; p. 197, Stephanie Stafford. All interior photos from Getty Images.

Typeset by Aptara, Inc.

ISBN 978-1-961442-56-6 (hardcover)
ISBN 978-1-965859-01-8 (epub)

Printed and bound in the United States of America

# Foreword

Cats have a reputation for being aloof and often contrarian, avoiding affection and often doing exactly what we *don't* want them to do. But people who live with cats get to see other sides of them, too: the ways that cats can be loving and deeply sensitive to their owners' emotions; the ways that they model persistence, survival, or clever solutions to difficult problems. Sometimes they reflect our own strengths and weaknesses back at us, prompting self-reflection—and, to the delight of our readers, inspiring our devotional writers to share their stories with us.

In this book we've collected one hundred of our favorite cat devotions from across three of Guideposts' most-loved devotionals: *Walking in Grace, Mornings with Jesus*, and, of course, the animal-themed devotional *All God's Creatures*. Some of these cats you'll meet only once, while in other cases you can follow their antics over the course of years as our authors describe their journeys together.

We hope these stories of love, hope, and faith will lift you up and brighten your devotional time—and perhaps even inspire an extra cuddle with your favorite feline.

Editors of *All God's Creatures*

# Relentless in Rescue

*I love the LORD, for he heard my voice; he heard my cry for mercy. Because he turned his ear to me, I will call on him as long as I live.*

—PSALM 116:1-2 (NIV)

As young newlyweds, we adopted Kimba, a pure white kitten with blue eyes. Special in many ways, he was a sweet little guy who loved to cuddle. Because he was deaf, Kimba meowed loudly and clung to us. I didn't mind.

His curiosity once got him in trouble. Through a hidden access, he managed to get between the walls of the bathtub, unable to find his way out.

We became aware of his predicament when we heard frantic cries coming from what sounded like the bathtub drain. After some confusion, we eventually found the entrance.

Kimba couldn't hear our calls, and the vibrations from us banging on the walls of the tub only frightened him. I tried a flashlight. Perhaps he'd come toward the glow.

No luck. He'd wedged himself too far back. "I'm going in," I told my wife.

Slithering on my belly, I inched between the walls of the tub. Stretching as far as possible, I grabbed Kimba and pulled him toward my chest. He immediately ran inside my shirt, safe and sound, purring with contentment. After my wife pulled me out by my ankles, we cleaned him up and made sure to Kimba-proof our home.

Kimba's escapade reminded me of Christ's relentless pursuit of us. The challenges of living in a fallen world often cause us to wander into the darkness. Lost and afraid, we call on the Lord. We may not hear his voice or see His light, but He is there, relentless in finding us and rescuing us. He will not give up until we are in His arms again.

*Tez Brooks*

***Father, may I never doubt Your love and care for me. Help me remember that, even in my farthest wanderings, I am never too far for You to find me. Amen.***

# A Nightly Visitor

***The righteous care for the needs of their animals.***
—PROVERBS 12:10 (NIV)

My husband, Brian, and I exchanged glances when we heard the meowing outside. The kitty was back. It had been appearing on the back porch of our apartment and whining until we came out. Then it would rub against our ankles, eager for a scratch behind the ears or a thorough belly rub.

As the weeks went on, we named the cat Olivia and brought her dishes of warm milk before bed. As a "dog person," I was surprised at my growing love for this kitty and eagerly looked forward to her nighttime visits.

Fall turned into winter, and it seemed too cold for a cat to live outdoors. But the apartment didn't allow us to keep pets. Our only option, it seemed, was to call the local animal patrol. It broke my heart to think of Olivia mewing all alone at night, hungry and cold.

A neighbor who had also become fond of Olivia called a few days later and said she had found a home for our nightly visitor—with a good family who had long wished for a pet. They came to collect Olivia on our porch that night.

Brian and I were heartbroken. "She will be so much happier with her new family than living outside," he said. I knew he was right.

I felt that I was getting a lesson straight from God's book of love. He, too, had loved and lost in order to allow much greater things to happen. *If I can feel this way about a cat*, I thought, *then I can only imagine the depth and strength of God's love for each of us.*

*Ashley Kappel*

***Lord, I'm always awed by the depth of Your love. Help others feel it, too.***

# **Arms of Love**

*There is no fear in love; but perfect love casts out fear.*
—1 JOHN 4:18 (NKJV)

A bolt of lightning flashed and then a deafening clap of thunder rattled the windows of my office. Our hypersensitive Manx cat, Barnie, dashed under my chair and let out pitiful yowls of fear at each crack and sharp clap of thunder. As an elderly cat, he usually ambled from room to room, but he became an Olympian track star when thunder rumbled or lightning flashed.

After leaning over the side of my chair and hyperextending my left arm, I managed to lift up my overweight black Manx. Usually, he would have gone feral on me. Although loving, Barnie was a rescued street cat who would take a swipe at anyone he felt was threatening him . . . including me, his cat "Papa."

My wife and I couldn't have kids, so we had cats. Barnie was my older boy. We had adopted him from a shelter. He and his three brothers were found abandoned in a shuttered manufacturing plant. We never knew what happened to his mother. Due to his fragile health, we almost lost him in the first months, but miraculously, he survived to become the big, strapping cat he was now.

"See?" I whispered in his ear, after parking him in my lap, his head nestled under my arm, "Papa's loving arms are around you now—you'll be just fine. Nothing can hurt you." He answered with a soft, guttural purr.

As I thanked the Lord for Barnie, I realized that Papa God was showing me what His love for me was like—so complete and encompassing that whenever I called upon Him, He was there, surrounding me with His loving presence.

*Terry Clifton*

***Lord, thank You for Your loving arms
that hold me whenever I need it.***

# Daddy Cat

***And if I go and prepare a place for you,***
***I will come back and take you to be with me.***
−JOHN 14:3 (NIV)

"Take his igloo and his bed. That's how he knows he's home." The man handed me the carrier with the old, feral cat. "His name is Daddy."

People without a place to live often take amazing care of the animals that find them in exchange for their unconditional love. Often strays can become their only true companions. That is how I met Daddy cat. He had been poisoned by the people who owned the property where he had lived, not by his caregivers, who loved him and had made sure he received his shots and neutering from a local program. Though his caregivers had no home of their own, they wanted to make sure that their Daddy cat would be safe and cared for when they said their tearful goodbyes. They left a bag of food for him when they had to leave the property.

Now he was mine. And just as the man had said, even though Daddy wandered at my farm, he would always find his way back to his igloo. Later, I went through a very difficult time and had to move. I packed up Daddy's igloo, and wherever I went, he was right at home with me and his mobile home. He reminded me that it wasn't *where* but *who* that made home feel like home. It wasn't long before this once-feral cat that had spent his life fending for himself begged to come inside. He learned that using a litter box and a soft cat bed were good things.

Daddy now loves spending mornings by my lap as I have coffee. He has allowed love to change him, and I have allowed him to change me. We both realize that home is where the love is. Trusting in a place to be home is not the same as trusting God to provide your safe place.

*Devon O'Day*

**I know that You are my shelter, God.
Help me remember that, no matter where I am.**

# Who Rescued Who?

*Blessed are those who mourn, for they will be comforted.*
—MATTHEW 5:4 (NIV)

I appreciate the irony of applying the term "empty-nest syndrome" to cat owners. But after the unexpected loss of our two aged felines within a month of each other, my husband and I couldn't deny the void in our hearts.

When a series of coincidences landed us at the local humane society, we decided to investigate the cats available for adoption. A ten-year-old tabby named Julie caught our attention, but we hesitated. How could we take on a new pet while still mourning the others? Surely someone else would choose her.

A week passed with Julie crowding my thoughts daily. After returning to the pet sanctuary, we requested details about her past. We learned Julie's world had been turned upside-down when one of her human parents died and the other had entered a memory-care facility. Her level of mourning eclipsed ours. This tiny cat had lost everything she'd ever known.

We brought her home that day. She's mended our hearts with laughter, surprising us with a joy we didn't think possible. I think of this verse: "A time to weep and a time to laugh, a time to mourn and a time to dance" (Ecclesiastes 3:4, NIV). Who knew those feelings could overlap? Jesus knows what we need to heal and grow in Him. He provides us opportunities to help others—even four-legged ones—as they suffer challenges similar to our own.

Rescue-pet owners often question who really did the rescuing, the owner or the animal. But the answer is Jesus.

*Heidi Gaul*

***Even in the midst of mourning, help me to open my heart to those in need, human or feline.***

# Of Feral Cats and Rehab

*They confronted me in the day of my disaster,*
*but the LORD was my support.*

–2 SAMUEL 22:19 (NIV)

Of the feral cats in my neighborhood, one in particular captures my attention. He is small and gray, with a notch at the tip of his right ear that indicates he'd been trapped, neutered, and released. At first, although I wanted to approach him, he'd always kept his distance.

I saw him sniffing about my yard on the day I received a difficult phone call. My friend was going into rehab. He'd called to explain that he'd be checking in right away. Although I was aware he'd had an alcohol problem in the past, I hadn't known it was still an issue. "I'm sorry I didn't tell you before," he said. "I guess I was just too afraid."

"I know it wasn't an easy decision," I said. "I'm here for you." As I got off the phone, Gray Cat crept up, his whiskers tickling my ankles. He, too, had once been nervous to approach me. After all, he'd had some bad breaks in life—he was abandoned and on his own. But I'd just stayed open until, after many weeks, he approached me. He let me scratch his ears.

God is like that for us too. He doesn't have to wait for us to tell him when we're in trouble—he already knows. He supports us, even when we've lost our way. Even when things are tough, he never abandons us. Sometimes he sends people to help. Like the organization that neuters feral cats. And the rehab place. We just have to be ready to accept the help, to lean into the strength that is always available from God above.

*Peggy Frezon*

*We are all imperfect, Lord, yet You love us equally. Allow me to be there for others in their times of need, just as You are always and forever here for us. Amen.*

# The Power of a Change of Perspective

*Do not conform to the pattern of this world, but be transformed by the renewing of your mind. Then you will be able to test and approve what God's will is— his good, pleasing and perfect will.*

—ROMANS 12:2 (NIV)

Our two cats, Sheba and Sooty, joined the family about five months apart. Their dislike for each other was immediate, with hissing, growling, and challenging each other for dominance. When we moved to a new house, one cat pretty much claimed the main level and one claimed the basement. However, the litter box and feeding area were in the basement, so they couldn't avoid each other altogether. I despaired that they would ever get along.

But then along came a new addition to the family—a rambunctious Lab puppy named Libby. Since she was young and trainable, I had hopes that she would get along well with the cats and maybe peace would reign. But no. Libby thought the cats were fun toys for her enjoyment and loved to chase them.

They did not appreciate her exuberance. In fact, we got to witness an amazing thing: the cats suddenly became a united front. They became Team Hate-the-Dog. They never again hissed at each other. They paired up and, with a few swats and lots of growling, successfully scared the new puppy away from their territory.

It's amazing what a change in perspective can do.

Sometimes failures and disappointments can make us think God has forgotten us. But down the road, we see that God was being merciful or was making a way for something even better in our lives. Sometimes it just takes a change of perspective to help us gain understanding, like Sheba and Sooty did when Libby came barging into their lives.

*Missy Tippens*

***God, help us to get out of our own heads, to get beyond our own problems and limited view of the world. Give us vision. Show us the world from Your perspective. Amen.***

# Kittens and Kiddies

*Even a child is known by his deeds, whether what he does is pure and right.*

—PROVERBS 20:11 (NKJV)

O ur church spent many Friday nights entertaining residents at the local nursing home with videos, homemade brownies, or musical performances. One particular Friday night, my friend Sharon brought a litter of kittens in a large wicker basket.

"Who would like to hold a kitten?" she asked.

Hands went up all over the room. The squirming balls of fluff and fur were a huge hit. Sharon gave the children the task of carrying the kittens from one person to the next. I smiled as I watched the young and old interacting with one another. It was obvious that the residents enjoyed talking with the children as much as they enjoyed stroking the kittens.

One little six-year-old girl scooped up a kitten and carried it over to a man slumped in his wheelchair.

"Would you like to pet the kitty too?" Katie asked. With her chubby hands, she thrust the kitten forward. The man hesitated before raising a finger, gnarled with arthritis, to stroke the animal's fuzzy head. "Look at its cute little nose," Katie babbled on.

The man's eyes became swimmy with tears when she plunked the kitten upon his lap and continued to talk about the adorableness of the animal's pink tongue and paws.

I felt a tight lump in my throat as I watched the little girl modeling Christlike concern for the older man—a stranger. I could hardly wait to tell Katie's parents and her Sunday school teacher that the seeds they had been sowing in the child's life had fallen upon fertile soil.

*Shirley Raye Redmond*

***Lord, this child is on the right path, but please watch over the others. Help make sure they know the way to go.***

# Everybody Gets Treats

***Follow God's example, therefore,
as dearly loved children.***

—EPHESIANS 5:1 (NIV)

The unmistakable sound of claws on metal interrupted my devotions. I stood up from the love seat, flung my hands in the air, and whined, "Again?" My eighteen-pound cat, Wally, stood on the back porch, gazing up at me. His emerald eyes held an angelic look. When I opened the door on a bright September day, Wally rushed to the counter where six pouches of cat treats stood. Each a different flavor.

A year before, when Wally was a kitten, I began the unwise habit of rewarding him with treats each time he was outside and returned home. Now he went outdoors at every opportunity. He knew those treats awaited him on his return.

I opened a yellow pouch and set a couple treats in front of Wally. Then I gave my other three cats the same reward. "Everybody gets treats!" I sang out. It seemed only fair to give the other "fur children" equal prizes, so they didn't feel left out. Or think Wally was my favorite.

Jesus tells a story in Matthew 20:1–16 about a landowner—representative of God—who paid all his workers equal wages, although some worked all day and others only an hour. The all-day helpers were angry at what they considered unfair treatment. But the landowner said, "Are you envious because I'm generous?" Ouch.

When I feel jealous of blessings God showers on new believers, I need to remind myself that God loves all His children with the same measure of love, no matter how long they've been His children. It's also a comfort to think that when I spoil my kitties, I'm imitating God.

*Jeanette Levellie*

*I know You're generous with all Your children. Remind me to find ways to be generous to others.*

# Changing Landscapes

***My God, my rock, in whom I take refuge . . .***
–2 SAMUEL 22:3 (RSV)

Our cat Chi weighed only fifteen ounces and was barely six weeks old when we brought her into our home in Los Angeles. No sooner had we done so than we started getting the house ready for an eventual sale.

For the first two years of Chi's life, we packed several boxes of "clutter" a week and moved them out to the garage. Books and bookcases vanished. Furniture changed location. Chi would hesitate in the doorway of a room as if she thought the floor might have changed too. We hoped she would realize we were the constant presence, even as the background shifted, but she was very nervous.

When we began showing the house, and strangers were coming in singly or in groups, Chi would have to be crated until they left. Repeated confinement was not to her liking. After a week the house sold and she was given her uninterrupted freedom again, but the packing accelerated.

The moving van showed up, and the house was suddenly empty. Chi was completely flummoxed.

On the two nights we spent in motels on our drive north, she wouldn't come out of her crate. And when we reached our new home, the entire upstairs was being remodeled, so we had to move into the basement for three months. She was just getting used to that when the upstairs was done, and we moved up there. Three years after that final move, Chi finally relaxed.

I, too, am hesitant when the landscape of my life keeps changing. And just as I hoped Chi would understand that we were still there, I tell myself that there's a constant for me. I just have to recognize God's presence.

*Rhoda Blecker*

***Help me not to forget that You're there,
Lord, no matter what else isn't.***

# A cat needs a place as much as it needs a person to make its own.

DORIS LESSING, NOVELIST

# Meowing for Love

***Beloved, if God so loved us, we ought
also to love one another.***

–1 JOHN 4:11 (KJV)

Our two cats, Tuxedo and Tiger, have been with us for a long time. Born in the same litter twelve years ago, they have moved with us through three states and have watched our three children grow. These cats are special members of our clan, though they have always lived outside. Fiercely independent, they roam their territory and fight their battles, but they are always home for supper.

Their appetites appear to have doubled, too. Now they stay around the back and meow for food every time the door is opened. Strangely, they often beg loudest when their bowls are brimming over with their favorite food. At first, such behavior perplexed me. For a while, I thought they might be having a problem with parasites, but our veterinarian assured me that was not the case.

Then one day, the explanation became perfectly clear. The only time I was ever able to pet these independent felines was when they were preoccupied with eating. But once they left their food bowls, they were impossible to catch. All of their lives, these cats had associated petting with eating. So now, when they want more affection, they feel that they have to beg for food in order to be petted.

I guess people are the same way. As a pastor, I hear a lot of folks complain about many things. But behind most of the laments, there is a deep hunger to be loved and appreciated. Wise is the person who can see through the crazy ways people ask to be stroked and then simply give them a pat on the head or a warm embrace. After all, they are not really hungry. Their plates are full. They are simply in need of love.

*Scott Walker*

*Help me recognize all the ways the people around me are asking to be loved, Lord, and show me the best way to care for them.*

# Blessed Assurance

***For you have been my hope, Sovereign LORD,
my confidence since my youth.***

−PSALM 71:5 (NIV)

**H**e's back! Old persistent Gray Cat. He turns up every morning and every evening for me to feed him. His piercing meow demands my attention, and if I don't respond immediately, he climbs up the back door. I don't know whose cat he is or if he really belongs to anyone, but he's pretty chubby for a stray. No doubt he dines at multiple homes in the neighborhood.

Gray Cat exudes confidence. I peer into those green eyes of his and see his complete assurance that I will feed him. And I do!

What would it be like to have absolute assurance that I would be cared for always? As a child, I remember singing the beloved hymn by Fannie J. Crosby, "Blessed Assurance, " which includes the line "Jesus is mine."

I love that thought: Jesus is *mine*! I've always believed I am His, but to consider Jesus being *mine* is almost more than I can fathom. There are so many people out there who need Jesus, who yearn for His love and attention. But still, if I reach out to Him, He is mine.

Words from the third stanza speak to me: *Perfect submission, all is at rest / I in my Savior am happy and blest / Watching and waiting, looking above / Filled with His goodness, lost in His love.* I can think of no place I'd rather be than lost in His love.

How I yearn to have the assurance of that gray cat. I want to spend more time resting in Jesus and His blessed assurance.

*Pat Butler Dyson*

*Perfect submission, all is at rest. I in my Savior am happy and blest . . .*

# I Know My Identity

***He is the One who loves us, who made us free
from our sins with the blood of his death.***
—REVELATION 1:5 (NCV)

I unashamedly spoil our four cats. I talk baby talk to them, sing them goofy songs, and give them too many treats.

I discovered my penchant for pets the autumn after I turned six. We'd recently moved into a new house. My brother, Danny, and I looked out our kitchen window that first Saturday morning and discovered five black-and-white kittens jumping in a pile of leaves. Danny beckoned Mom to the window.

"Uh-oh," she said. "Those aren't cats. They're skunks."

Mom called animal control to catch the critters, and we eventually adopted a kitten. I've been a cat lover ever since.

As an adult, I can now easily distinguish a cat from a skunk. But I'm not always as smart with identifying myself. I might base my value on a comment someone makes, whether I prayed that day or not, or how tight my favorite blouse is.

Yet in my heart, I know my true identity lies in my relationship with Jesus. What He thinks of me and what

He says about me is God's reality. And because of Jesus's lavish sacrifice, I know He thinks I'm the cat's meow.

*Jeanette Levellie*

***On the bad days when I forget my own worth,
Lord, remind me of who I really am.***

# Chasing the Wrong Light

**Now godliness with contentment is great gain.**
—1 TIMOTHY 6:6 (NKJV)

My son Henry shines a flashlight on the living room rug. He flicks the beam of light back and forth until he rouses our cat Frank, who jumps up out of a sound sleep and pounces on the radiant circle. Henry laughs, picking up the pace. With a quick twist of the wrist, he casts the light the distance of the room. "Go, Frank! Go!" Henry squeals.

I scan the circulars that have come with the morning's newspaper. There are lots of toys the boys want for Christmas. An expensive food processor that's out of my price range would be great for me, since the one I have only works on one setting. There's a set of plates that catches my eye. *How wonderful it would be to have a perfect, full set for when we have company!*

Henry slows the pace of flashing and shines the light back and forth. Frank's paws meet the beam, and he puts his face right in the center. Exhausted, Frank lies down and Henry, tired of playing, puts down the flashlight.

I look up from the newspaper just as a scrap of sun shines through the window. Frank runs to that too. He settles down right in the light, closes his eyes and stretches to show his belly. He looks so peaceful; I put down the paper and join him.

In the warmth of the sun, I listen to Frank purr and my mind turns to the sales circular. I sometimes make the mistake of thinking something I buy will make me content; energy spent chasing the wrong light.

*Sabra Ciancanelli*

*Dear Lord, You are the Source of contentment. Help me to bask in Your true light.*

# Lost Kitten—Found Hope

***Cast your cares on the LORD and he will sustain you;
he will never let the righteous be shaken.***

—PSALM 55:22 (NIV)

Misha was a palm-size Siamese kitten who appeared one night in a torrential downpour while I was making a deposit at the bank. At first, I thought she was an illusion. But those blue eyes and that cry proved her real, and I decided to take her home with me.

I thought I was saving a little feline waif, but she was the one who would rescue my drowning spirit. I decided to take her with me to a cabin on Monteagle Mountain in Tennessee on my getaway weekend. Sometime during the night, the pressure of a warm room and the cold outside opened the door just a crack, and my tiny cat escaped into the dark.

I panicked when I woke up and realized my little friend was gone. Management and cabin guests called and searched, but Misha didn't appear, and I returned home devastated. Through tears, I gave her to God. I wrote her name on a small scrap of paper and put it in a ceramic hand on my nightstand. Each time I saw the

32

paper, it reminded me that she was in God's hands. I gave up my worry and my control to the one who had brought her to me.

Three weeks later, I got a call from the cabin office. Misha had been found crying next to the warmth of a hot tub on the premises. That sweet homecoming reminded me that giving our hopeless causes to God is not puffery or empty words but the most powerful thing we can do. The symbol of writing a prayer and placing it in a specific holding place reminds us to continue to release those tightly held hurts to him.

From missing cats to broken hearts, putting our hope in the hands of the one who loves us brings a peace that surpasses understanding and hope where there is none.

*Devon O'Day*

**I know everything is safe in Your hands, from the tiniest kitten to my own heart.**

# A New View

***I will praise You, for I am fearfully and wonderfully made; marvelous are Your works.***
—PSALM 139: 14 (NKJV)

**M**y husband, Terry, and I took in a stray kitten and named him Midnight. Instead of sleeping in his new luxury cat bed, Midnight insisted on sleeping in our bedroom windowsill, next to a big tree outside the window. *Why is he drawn to that tree?* I wondered.

One night, after Midnight settled onto the windowsill, I got my answer. It was in the form of an unkempt, scraggly-looking little possum hanging upside-down. And it was looking right back at me!

Why was our new cat was drawn to this long-snouted creature? What did Midnight see in his friend? Had they met during Midnight's former life on the street? My imagination had a field day with that thought.

My evenings spent watching Midnight and his upside-down friend changed my view of him—and me. The possum hanging upside down, which initially bothered me, no longer did. I did some research and discovered that only young possums hang by their tails. Our temporary visitor was a baby, just like our Midnight. There was a bond between these two creatures that went beyond the window and beyond how each looked.

Getting to know the sensitive and unique ways of the little possum made me aware of how God made me to be just me and not stamped from a cookie cutter. We are all made for a purpose, and each one of God's creatures is the beautiful, unique expression of a loving God.

*Sandra Clifton*

***Loving Lord, thank You for placing beautiful creatures in my life. I am thankful for the gift of Your unique creatures that warm my heart and teach me something. Amen.***

# Fear of Change

*However, as it is written: "What no eye has seen, what no ear has heard, and what no human mind has conceived"—the things God has prepared for those who love him.*

–1 CORINTHIANS 2:9 (NIV)

**M**oving is difficult—physically and emotionally. Leaving the known for the unknown is daunting. During one of our moves, we had a particularly difficult time with one of our pets. We were moving out of one parsonage into another, which meant a specific move day and time.

We had the timing planned perfectly. I put our indoor cats in the bathroom in the basement and put a sign on the door to keep out. Everything went great. The moving van left, and we finished the last-minute loading of our cars. Once it was time to leave, we went to put the cats in their carriers.

But one thing we hadn't counted on was how the noise had affected them. When we opened the bathroom door, they shot out and hid. We couldn't find them anywhere! Finally, Sheba came to us, but the time had arrived when we were supposed to be out of the house, and we still could not find Sooty. After about an hour of calling and searching, we finally heard her meow. She was in the rafters of the unfinished part of the basement. We found a ladder, and our son (her favorite person) eventually coaxed her down.

I have to admit, despite the excitement of our future, I felt a little bit like Sooty. None of us likes change. We cling to the comfort of the familiar. But God desires more for us than we can ever imagine. No matter how scary change can be, God enables us to move forward and equips us for an amazing future.

*Missy Tippens*

*God, thank You for coming with me,
no matter where I go.*

# The Unexpected Hitchhiker

***You are the God who performs miracles;
you display your power among the peoples.***
—PSALM 77:14 (NIV)

*W*hen did this stroller get so heavy? I looked at my then two-year-old son, Nathan. Had he grown since our last walk to the store?

I was in the produce department when I heard a *meow*.

"Nathan, are you being a kitty today?" It was such a realistic impression.

He leaned over the edge of his stroller. "Kitty."

I heard another meow, but this one did not come from Nathan. I followed his finger to the storage basket under his stroller and gasped. "Oh no."

Lucia, my tortoiseshell calico, had decided to nap in the stroller basket. The only thing keeping her from escaping was my purse. How had shoving it in not woken her up? How had we made it all the way to the store without her running off? *God, please don't let her get out. Please, please.* Now aware of her surroundings, Lucia started whining. A lady gave me a look. I smiled back, hoping she wasn't allergic. "The cat stowed away."

I prayed the whole way to the checkout stand and the whole walk home, listening to Lucia's cries of distress. Every friend who heard the story laughed out loud. Because the story ended well, I was able to laugh too.

At the time, my family was in financial stress after a health crisis. We needed a miracle. That day, our miracle was that Lucia didn't escape in the grocery store or along the road. The memory of my frantic prayers became a reminder that God heard me. If He could keep a cat in a stroller for almost an hour, He could do just about anything.

*Jeanette Hanscome*

***Lord, You truly are the God who works miracles. Help me to recognize them and trust Your power and grace. Thank You for hearing me and caring and for Your constant reminders that You are at work. Amen.***

# Misty, Then and Now

*Finally, brothers and sisters, whatever is true, whatever is noble, whatever is right, whatever is pure, whatever is lovely, whatever is admirable—if anything is excellent or praiseworthy—think about such things.*

—PHILIPPIANS 4:8 (NIV)

The last time I saw Mom's cat, Misty, things were different. In the past, the little gray feline would stop in her tracks, hiss, and run off to hide.

Misty was a kitten when Mom got her, and those early formative months for socialization weren't happy ones. Mom's second husband had cast a negative shroud over the household. His misguided attempts to manage the kitten resulted in him shooing her away whenever she got underfoot and trying to chase her out of corners. The poor little kitten spent most of her time hiding under the bed.

Now Mom lives alone, and the home at last feels peaceful and harmonious. This is evident in the change in Misty. I recently arrived from out of state for a visit. When I walked into the house, she calmly looked at me and swished her tail. As I approached, she even took a step toward me and leaned into my stroke.

"Mom! This is the first time in sixteen years she let me pet her," I said. "It's wonderful to see her so happy."

When our home is stressful, even our pets can feel it. The same is true for me when I surround myself with negativity, such as crowded schedules, an unhealthy diet, or toxic people. God's Word reminds me to surround myself with things that are positive, uplifting, and beautiful. Focusing my mind on such things transforms me from pessimistic and discouraged to positive and hopeful, just as a peaceful setting transformed Misty from an anxious kitten to a trusting adult cat.

*Peggy Frezon*

***Help me identify the influences I don't need in my life, Lord, and lead me toward the things I need to focus on.***

# Fearful Ivy

*"Peace I leave with you; my peace I give you. I do not give to you as the world gives. Do not let your hearts be troubled and do not be afraid."*

—JOHN 14:27 (NIV)

My cat Ivy is terrified of our new rescue kitty, Julie. Though Julie is geriatric and small, the younger one can't bear her. Ivy's afraid to share me with this sweet old girl, as if she thinks I can't love them both. Now Ivy won't come into the house, leaving me to wonder if this four-legged war will ever end.

There have been times when I've walked in Ivy's padded feet, frightened of something beyond my control. I couldn't bear to admit it's *all* out of my control. Jesus was, is, and will be the One in charge. He protects me from trouble, even when it's of my own making— especially of my own making.

Like Ivy worrying that we'll stop caring about her and favor Julie, I've forgotten Christ has love enough for me and everyone else in the world. It's limitless. Why have I allowed myself to be threatened by His tenderness toward others?

My husband and I are keeping a close eye on these pets, maneuvering them toward some sort of truce. This morning Ivy came up from the basement for a few minutes, so we could brush her and fuss over her. It's a start. When she's ready, we'll be able to restore peace in our home.

Like my husband and I waiting for our scaredy-cat to trust us, Jesus is patient. Whenever I'm ready to surrender to His wisdom, He stills my fears and guides me back to His peace. He always has and always will.

*Heidi Gaul*

**Sometimes my fears get the better of me, Jesus. Please remind me to trust You.**

One never ceases to find new wonders in a cat. Pattern and swirl of fur, elegance of movement, perfection of form. Delicacy of whisker, brilliance of eye, gentleness of outstretched paw and loving, butting head.

PAM BROWN, AUTHOR

# Lily the Sphynx

*"The LORD does not look at the things people look at. People look at the outward appearance, but the LORD looks at the heart."*

—1 SAMUEL 16:7 (NIV)

When I think of a kitten, most often my mind's eye imagines a short-legged, round-faced, fluffy bundle of fur. My niece Katie has always wanted a different breed of cat in her life. And her husband, James, gave her the delight of her heart one Valentine's Day. Her gift was Lily, a sphynx, also known as a hairless cat. Lily's triangular head, huge ears, wide-set eyes, and sleek, muscular body endeared her to the family in no time at all.

Some cat breeds hold themselves aloof from their humans, but sphynx are friendly, almost doglike in their attraction to people. They are sweet and smart, and Lily is no exception. But what Lily knows, perhaps better than anything else, is how precious she is to the family. Katie and James's daughter, Elizabeth, adores her, and while the gift was for Katie, the cat has become Elizabeth's baby. Elizabeth is convinced that Lily is the cutest thing ever and is shocked to think that some people may feel otherwise.

To be honest, I think hairless cats are pretty funny looking (maybe not *ugly,* but funny). And to be even more honest, I am not all that pleased with the way I look. It is in my nature to be very critical of the view as I look into a mirror. My hair is too fine, my face is too round . . . But what God sees when He looks at me is His precious, beloved daughter. He knows me inside and out. He loves me with an everlasting love. And that love is shaping me into a beautiful reflection of my heavenly Father.

*Liz Kimmel*

***Thank You, Father, that You see every part of us and love us as no one else can. Help me to stop striving for outer beauty. I trust that You will pour Your beautiful nature into and through me, that I might bless those I interact with daily. Amen.***

# When Love Casts Out Fear

*That you, being rooted and grounded in love, may have strength to comprehend with all the saints what is the breadth and length and height and depth, and to know the love of Christ that surpasses knowledge, that you may be filled with all the fullness of God.*

—EPHESIANS 3:17-19 (ESV)

**"S**he's too feral." The humane shelter employee went on to inform me that the cat I had captured would be euthanized if I left her.

I blinked back tears as I hefted the carrier that housed the frightened feline and trudged to my car. Were death or a life of danger in the wild the only options for this beautiful calico?

But an experienced source almost begged, "Don't return her to the wild." She assured me feral cats can be rehabilitated. I grabbed at the hope. I wanted this precious cat to be free from a life of fear.

I was careful not to rush the rehabilitation process, though eager to show her how much I loved her. One day, I reached a finger through the bars of her large crate and touched her soft fur. She didn't startle. Instead, she stayed near, and I extended a few more fingers to pet her.

Breakthrough. She leaned into the petting, and her life changed. My touch had shattered the wall of fear surrounding her. After that day, I could help her confront anything frightening simply by stroking her, as if my love flowed into her and came out as courage.

When I look at my rescued cat, I see a reflection of myself. How many times have I relied on fear instead of God to keep me safe? How often have I tried to conquer my fears without God's help? I often let fear drive me away from God, but He's waiting for me to draw close so He can show me just how much He loves me.

*Jerusha Agen*

**Lord, when I am afraid, remind me to draw near to You. Touch me with Your love. Let it flow through me and come out as courage. Amen.**

# I Know What I Saw

***Now faith is confidence in what we hope for
and assurance about what we do not see.***

—HEBREWS 11:1 (NIV)

I have a history of seeing wild animals in strange places. My family has a history of not believing me. Like the time I saw a mountain lion outside my tent in Big Bend National Park, Texas, or when I saw a panther on a golf green. They didn't see what I saw, so they would say, "You're imagining things."

They always made me doubt my experience until I saw the jaguarundi. We were fishing on the southern Texas coast. As the sun rose, my husband waded off after a redfish. Half-awake, I gazed at the shore. A primitive-looking big cat scooted through the tall grass. Its back sloped down toward a small, flat head, and its thick tail waved powerfully over the brush. What was it?

"A coyote," my husband said when I told him about it. I insisted that it was a primitive cat.

"OK, maybe a bobcat," he said. No. I knew what I had seen, and it was a very special creature.

I described it to the old-timers at the tackle store. "Sounds like a jaguarundi," they said. They got excited and told us about this endangered creature that moves like a weasel, swims, and leaps from trees to capture prey. Jaguarundi are considered extinct in Texas, but we agreed: I wasn't imagining it. The old-timers had seen them in the past. Even though no one had encountered one here recently, I had seen one too.

Their faith helped me trust that my experience was real. Others may doubt my encounters, but when I talk with those who understand, I am strengthened. I have felt God's presence in my life. I have seen a jaguarundi. It doesn't matter what anyone else thinks. I know what I saw.

*Lucy H. Chambers*

**Dear Lord, help us to know You and recognize Your presence in our lives. Provide us with friends who can help us hold on to our faith, even when others doubt. Amen.**

# Fishing for Smiles

*"Be strong and courageous. Do not be afraid or terrified because of them, for the LORD your God goes with you; he will never leave you nor forsake you."*

—DEUTERONOMY 31:6 (NIV)

Cranky was the most unusual male cat I had ever adopted—half Siamese, half Manx. He was gorgeous, with long back legs, short fur, and no tail. His markings and crystal-blue eyes were all Siamese, but his attitude was 100 percent cranky. Thinking I could cheer him up, I put him on a leash for a walk outside.

What a scaredy-cat. Even the breeze spooked him. He hissed, and if he'd had a tail, it would have puffed out. Back indoors, I trashed the leash, but he still growled. To help Cranky adjust, I gave him extra treats and lots of attention. But at the slightest noise, he bolted under my bed. Cranky seemed afraid of life itself.

One day, I tied a toy mouse to the end of a fishing pole and stood in the yard casting. Cranky eyed the moving target, wiggling his cute tailless rear end in readiness. As the line sailed out, Cranky leaped at least five feet into the air and nabbed the mouse on the first try. And the second and third tries. Over the next weeks, Cranky's crabbiness faded. He stopped hissing and delighted me with his loud purr. Every afternoon, he would stand by the door, eager for another round of catfishing.

It made me think of all the times I've grumped my way through life. Usually, my crankiness stems from fear—fear I'm not good enough, fear that others will hurt me, fear I won't make it. Although I try not to hiss at anyone, I smile more when I remember that God loves me and will never abandon me. These days, if Cranky Cat gets grumpy, we still go outside for a little catfishing. Before you know it, we're both in better moods.

*—Linda S. Clare*

***May I be led by the dreams in my heart, not pushed around by the fears in my mind.***

# We Weren't Going to Get Another Cat

***I will save the lame, and gather those who were driven out.***

−ZEPHANIAH 3:19 (NKJV)

We were not going to get another cat. Two were enough, especially since our cats were always "inside only" cats, and the house was just not that big. We already shared it with Tau, nineteen, and Chi, nearly nine. Besides, our dog Hobo weighed seventy-five pounds and would likely intimidate a new animal.

Then a tortoiseshell kitten wandered up the driveway. She was a tiny little thing, but not in bad shape. We tried to ignore her.

The kitten moved onto our deck, and suddenly all the birds we fed regularly were in some peril. So we were forced to feed her to keep her from chasing them. And every time we took food out to her, she meowed and purred and rubbed against us and was generally too adorable for words. We didn't so much weaken as fall completely apart, resolutions forgotten. We took her to the vet, got a clean bill of health, and brought her home.

We named her L.E.—short for Lambda Epsilon, because all of our other cats were named after Greek letters, but the shorter version fit her better.

We were warned that because she'd been an outdoor cat, she would always try to escape. To our surprise, she not only didn't want to go out, but she took over the house. In two days, she knew every room, every stick of furniture; it was all hers. Oh, she liked to look out the windows, but it was clear that being inside and part of our family had been her goal from the beginning.

It's still a bit of a battle. Tau is too old to play, and he lets her know that with no hesitation when she tries to entice him. Chi would rather the kitten caught fire; there is much hissing and growling when she comes anywhere near her. And Hobo is upset at being bossed around by a five-pound cat. But we're all adjusting.

*Rhoda Blecker*

**We are grateful for the reminder, God, that Your plans always make ours look puny.**

# Rescuing Mushu

*"Because he loves me," says the LORD, "I will rescue him; I will protect him, for he acknowledges my name."*
—PSALM 91:14 (NIV)

Fifty feet up in a tree, Mushu sought safety from a dog. The louder the dog barked, the higher he climbed, until he couldn't make his way down again.

Neighbors said he'd come down when he got hungry, thirsty, or cold. But three days passed, and Mushu remained in the tree. Knowing a storm was brewing, his owners called the fire department, but their ladder couldn't reach him. Night fell, bringing with it seventy-mile-per-hour winds, rain, and chilling temperatures.

As soon as the sun peeked over the horizon, Mushu's owners rushed outside. Miraculously, the cat still clung to his branch, but they knew the situation was critical.

"What about an arborist?" a neighbor suggested. "Maybe he could get Mushu down."

The next morning, the tree expert arrived. Moving slowly to minimize the clank of his equipment, the arborist began his climb. As he neared the branch where the frightened animal huddled, the cat stirred. But instead of moving away from him, he crept closer. Soon the climber was close enough to reach out.

"Come here, Mushu," he said softly. "Come to me."

On wobbly paws, Mushu inched toward his rescuer until he was safe in his embrace.

Mushu's rescue reminds me a lot of mine. Trapped in my sin from which I had no hope of escaping, I was powerless to change myself or my circumstances. Then a kind friend introduced me to Jesus. On wobbly faith, I inched toward Him until I was safe in His embrace. And Jesus has carried me ever since.

*Lori Hatcher*

*Father, thank You for sending Jesus to be our rescuer. And thank You that He's so much more than that—He's a counselor, comforter, advocate, and friend. Amen.*

# Flying Cats

*Abram believed the LORD, and he credited
it to him as righteousness.*

—GENESIS 15:6 (NIV)

Farm cats and farm kittens are incredibly gifted at survival. They are born with the intrinsic belief that they can catch and feed themselves because the ability is within them. The thought that they may not be able to sustain themselves doesn't occur to them. There is no social media to compare lives with other, more successful cats. They just patiently do what is within them to live.

Tigre was a feral kitten, part of a litter from a cat that just showed up at my farm. Fed well, she still hunted like a professional from a very early age. She was a climber almost instantly. I watched her sleep in a tree right outside my window, realizing she was preparing her hunting ground. She slept there and became part of the environment, so birds would eventually become used to her and not even see her.

I thought it was cute that she thought she could actually catch a bird in a tree. I mean, cats can't fly. Can they?

I would watch her watching birds. She didn't make a move as she studied them. *She won't ever catch one, will she?*

Then one day, I found the evidence of a bird she had caught. She had brought the bird to her littermates, and her survival skills had won their dinner. I could not believe that she was successful in such a difficult task. But she clearly had not doubted her own ability. She believed in what her inner self knew.

We all have inner survival skills and a Creator who has equipped us for unbelievable things. When I patiently wait for God to move me to use the skills with which He has equipped me, then move boldly and believe in my skills, I will be successful in His plan for me.

*Devon O'Day*

**God, move me past any doubt of Your belief in me, past the unbelief of those around me, into the success You have waiting for me. In Jesus's name. Amen.**

# Millions of Blessings

*"Give, and it will be given to you. A good measure, pressed down, shaken together and running over, will be poured into your lap. For with the measure you use, it will be measured to you."*
—LUKE 6:38 (NIV)

When my kids were little, one of their favorite books was *Millions of Cats*. Being a cat lover, I never minded reading it again. But recently, when I saw a local news report, my heart broke. Four hundred cats had been discovered on a woman's property. She had tried to care for the kitties by herself until she was hospitalized. I watched in sadness as disease-ridden and starving cats roamed the rural yard.

Some blamed the woman for hoarding felines and allowing them to breed. But one of the woman's relatives cradled a calico kitty and begged for donations of cat food and medicine. Still, I fretted. I sent in a small sum, but it felt like a drop in a very big bucket. Surely, God wouldn't abandon these innocent creatures?

A few weeks later, I was watching my young grandchildren when a follow-up report announced that several organizations had come to the kitties' rescue. The same relative held a bright-eyed ginger tabby, thanked those who had offered help, and vowed to find homes for all four hundred cats. My three-year-old granddaughter pointed to the TV. "I like that one and that one and that one!" Her older brother added, "Can we get some?"

I hugged them and smiled, knowing my own weakness for strays. "Maybe," I answered. I couldn't help thinking that whenever I feel my life's problems spiraling out of control, God always helps me find a way out. Instead of leaving me with four hundred problems to solve, God can turn a bunch of troubles into hundreds of little blessings—including the two blessings sitting next to me. I switched off the TV and pulled out our dog-eared copy of *Millions of Cats*.

*Linda S. Clare*

***Thank You for showing me how problems can become opportunities for love.***

# Bubble over My Head

***For I know the thoughts that I think
toward you, says the LORD.***

—JEREMIAH 29:11 (NKJV)

Once again, Rudy, our cat, had outsmarted me. I had no choice but to leave a message on our vet's answering machine: "We have to cancel Rudy's appointment this morning. We can't find him." I had a project deadline. I was too busy for this.

Actually, I knew where Rudy was. He had defied physics by flattening his overweight body and wiggling his way under our oversized couch. We had taken every precaution that morning. We followed our usual routine—had coffee, watched the morning news, and did not even broach the subject of Rudy's appointment. But somehow, he knew. "I am convinced that I must have this comic-book speech bubble over my head," I said in frustration, "that allows him to read our plans."

With Rudy, this information bubble seemed to continually hover above my head. And it gave Rudy the "upper paw": *Mr. Terry is going to the kitchen to feed me; he is heading to his recliner, but I shall occupy it first; he is planning to clip my nails, so I will hide.* Was this apparent mind-reading a natural thing for a cat? Or did I just need therapy? *Lord, how can this cat foresee my every move?*

But as I thought about it, I realized that it wasn't about mind-reading at all—just as I follow God closely, attentive to the signals that He sends, my cat pays close attention to my body language and actions.

I saw Rudy with new eyes. His being one step ahead of me was a sign of God's loving hand in creating a pet that loved me and was, in his own cat ways, in sync with me.

*Terry Clifton*

*Lord, I want to always be in sync with Your will. Help me keep my eyes on You—even on my off days.*

I love cats because
I enjoy my home; and
little by little, they
become its visible soul.

JEAN COCTEAU, POET AND PLAYWRIGHT

# Enough

*And God is able to make all grace abound toward you,
that you, always having all sufficiency in all things,
may have an abundance for every good work.*
–2 CORINTHIANS 9:8 (NKJV)

Libby thought she was a night owl, not a calico cat. It never failed. Once I got myself tucked into bed for the night, she would jump up and pace back and forth along the length of my body, as if she were walking on the boardwalk. When she neared my face, she purred and begged me to pet her. Then she would walk back down the boardwalk toward my feet and curl up next to me as if I were her heater. She knew how to get comfortable. Repeat over and over. Then all of a sudden, just when I thought the petting had fulfilled her needs, she would jump off the bed to run and have a bite to eat. She sought satisfaction and found it in being petted, in being comfortable, and in being fed, but never for long!

I'm a lot like that, if I'm being honest. I seek satisfaction through temporary fixes. I desire comfort. I gain a wanted possession and realize it doesn't really fill the void the way I thought it would. And I seek to be "petted," too, in the form of praise or attention. Even when others give me the recognition I think I need or deserve, I'm not satisfied. And just like Libby, once I realize the comfort-seeking isn't fulfilling me, I go to comfort food to make me feel better.

When I evaluate the "why" behind my dissatisfaction, I realize it's because only God is enough. Only God can fill a God-size void. My heavenly Father has been there all the time, wanting to meet my needs. He sent the Comforter to be my comfort. He whispers words of affirmation to my soul. He provides spiritual bread that leaves me feeling full. What more could I want?

*Kathy Carlton Willis*

***Dear Lord, may I find "soul-fill-ment" that goes beyond fulfillment as I receive Your comfort, affirmation, and provision. You are enough. Amen.***

# Baby Girl

*Praise be to the God and Father of our Lord Jesus Christ, the Father of compassion and the God of all comfort, who comforts us in all our troubles, so that we can comfort those in any trouble with the comfort we ourselves receive from God.*

—2 CORINTHIANS 1:3–4 (NIV)

During a recent visit with my friend Susy, I was introduced to their many animals, including a beautiful calico named Baby Girl.

"You won't see much of her," Susy's husband, Robert, told me. Susy added that they had rescued the calico from an animal hoarder and the cat avoided everyone except their daughter.

Then Baby Girl slinked over. I've always been a cat lover, so I couldn't resist kneeling down to say hello, prepared for her to ignore me. She brushed against my hand.

"Wow," Robert said. "That never happens."

All week long, I felt drawn to Baby Girl. I remembered what it felt like to be suspicious of people while recovering from some traumatic experiences. The friends I treasured most had patiently drawn me out of my cocoon. I tried to do the same with Baby Girl, greeting her in the morning and whenever I saw her outside, letting her come and go on her terms.

One day, while sitting on the porch, I felt her paw on my leg. I reached down and touched her head. "Hey, Baby Girl." She stretched both paws up to my knee, then she hopped on to my lap, curled up, and started to purr. My heart melted as I stroked her.

My bond with Baby Girl felt like God's way of pointing out a gift I had gained from painful experience: the ability to give others what I had once needed—friendship, affection, and patience. It was one more reminder to never forget the comfort God provides so I can pass it on to someone else.

*Jeanette Hanscome*

**God, is there someone in my life who needs extra patience right now? Show me an act of kindness I can do for them.**

# Ivy the Hunter

***Accept one another, then, just as Christ accepted you, in order to bring praise to God.***

—ROMANS 15:7 (NIV)

Cats. I love them. So, when a nearby farmer needed a home for a barn cat's female kitten, I volunteered. The thought of that tiny bundle snuggling on my lap drew me in like a cat to yarn.

But Ivy, an independent calico, soon let me know there would be none of that nonsense. She had a job to do and intended to do it. Even at six weeks, she hunted her prey—the unsuspecting earthworms. Daily, I'd find them wiggling on the floor and return them to the soil, sprinkled with my apologies. As she grew, her hunt continued. Mice, voles, and the odd gopher met their match—and their Maker—at her acquaintance.

It's been five years, and she's yet to cuddle with me. I doubt she ever will. Ivy isn't the purring companion I'd expected. Instead, Jesus gave me a half-pint teacher. And the lessons I'm learning are heavier than her seven pounds.

Ivy doesn't live according to my whims but lives according to the way Jesus made her. She knows who she is and lives her life to that purpose. Whether I approve or not. As I glance out the window, I spot her chasing a leaf, the embodiment of joyful well-being.

And then I understand. In the same way I've accepted her, Jesus loves me—just as I am. I don't have to be anything but true to Him and myself. As with Ivy, my purpose and worth aren't dependent on pleasing others. I've found myself in Christ, and that's enough. I'm enough. And like my small but fierce cat, I'm complete.

*Heidi Gaul*

***Let me learn from the cats in my life to accept myself and my life with grace, and to see myself as Jesus sees me.***

# Pecked by Problems

*That is why, for Christ's sake, I delight in weaknesses, in insults, in hardships, in persecutions, in difficulties. For when I am weak, then I am strong.*

—2 CORINTHIANS 12:10 (NIV)

I had a powerful cat named Tarzan. Snow white and sleek, he was fearless. He dozed in the dappled sunlight under a big oak, and the blue jays and other birds gave our yard a wide berth.

Then Tarzan had an accident. A car hit him and broke his leg. When it healed, nerve damage left him lame. He couldn't run or hunt as he had before. Now more than anything, he wanted to relax in the sunshine.

The blue jays saw he was wounded. They came back and began pecking at him. For a few days, I kept rushing out to shoo them away. But Tarzan didn't panic. He walked around the yard, dragging his lame leg until the blue jays came closer. Then he leaned back on his good leg, leaped up, and caught one. Blue feathers flew, and soon, Tarzan napped contentedly under the tree.

How often do I blame setbacks for keeping me from living the life that I desire? When I see Tarzan keeping the blue jays at bay, I remember that everything that happens can be used for good. Yes, others may torment me, and old ways of coping may not work anymore. My strength will fail. But my weaknesses offer opportunities to draw closer to God, who will provide new understanding and new ways to deal with the incessant pecking of life's challenges.

*Lucy H. Chambers*

*Dear Creator, life knocks me down in so many ways. Problems arise just when I feel the least able to cope. But when I am weak, You are strong. When I feel damaged, help me trust that You will reveal a path forward that brings me closer to You. Grant me strength to face each day just as I am and grace to bask in the warmth of Your love. Amen.*

# Persistent in Prayer

***Then Jesus told his disciples a parable to show them that they should always pray and not give up.***

—LUKE 18:1 (NIV)

Our cat, Earl, was not at his usual place at the door one morning, demanding to be fed. I wasn't particularly concerned, but as the day wore on and Earl didn't appear, I worried. I beseeched Jesus to send the feisty stray, whom we'd adopted a few years earlier, home.

Night fell and still no Earl. I put a picture of him on a lost pet Facebook page. I walked around the neighborhood calling his name. I put flyers in nearby mailboxes.

I barely slept as I begged Jesus to send Earl home. The next morning, I hurried to the door, but Earl wasn't there. All day long, I searched, called, and prayed.

By the third morning, Earl had still not appeared. With a heavy heart, I gave up and stopped praying. Earl was gone for good.

My daily devotion that morning addressed Jesus's parable about the persistent widow who pleaded with the unfair judge to grant justice against her adversary.

She kept praying, never gave up, and finally, the judge granted her request (Luke 18:1–8).

This *Jesus nudge* was a message to me. I couldn't give up, either. I called the area animal shelters and resumed my prayers for Earl's return.

Early the next morning, my husband hollered, "He's back!"

Earl had been trapped in a neighbor's garage. They'd been out of town, and when they'd returned, Earl quickly escaped. I hurriedly shook kibble into his bowl, as I thanked Jesus for bringing Earl home and for teaching me to never give up in prayer.

*Pat Butler Dyson*

***Lord, is there a prayer I gave up on too soon? Remind me to trust Your timing.***

# Gentle Spirits

***My dear brothers, take note of this: Everyone should be
quick to listen, slow to speak and slow to become angry.***
—JAMES 1:19 (NIV)

Olivia is a cat with a gentle spirit. I have never seen her hiss at a dog, even one chasing her. She doesn't demand our attention. She just quietly sits near, her very presence ushering in a feeling of calm. She was a feral foundling but showed up in our lives with this gentle spirit. She seemed to know that to have her needs met, she didn't need to fight for everything. She just allows good to come to her.

Her manner was contagious. Dogs wreaking havoc would quickly lose interest and go to their beds and lie down. Other cats would not defend their territory because Olivia didn't challenge them for space. She lives in the mindset that there is always enough. Peace follows Olivia wherever she goes.

I want to have more of that peace-bearing gentle spirit. Often, I have felt challenged in the workplace. People vie for a place at the top. We get jealous. We get angry. We harbor resentment. Even if we say nothing about those emotions, they show in our countenance.

When faced with confrontation of late, I have begun the practice of remaining quiet. When allowed to speak, I take my time and consider compassion before responding. Instead of reacting quickly, I take a few moments to allow God to form my sentences. I have learned that when I allow gentleness to enter the room, the confrontation usually diffuses and peace falls on heated moments. Quiet and compassionate truth always leaves the most powerful impact.

*Devon O'Day*

**God, when I'm in conflict, whisper words into my heart that help me enter the room in peace.**

# What're You Gonna Do about It?

*"Submit to God and be at peace with him;*
*in this way prosperity will come to you."*
—JOB 22:21 (NIV)

Ever since she was a kitten, I've played with my cat, Zoe, by picking her up and gently turning her on her back, then blowing on her tummy, just like many parents do with their small children. Zoe struggled a little at first, but I'd hold her in my arms and say, "What're you gonna do about it?" and then blow on her furry tummy again.

It didn't take long for Zoe to figure out that when she heard me say, "What're you gonna do about it?" there was no point in struggling. In fact, when I'd say, "What're you gonna do about it?" Zoe would go completely limp, from her ears to the tip of her tail, and meekly submit to having her tummy snuffled. Once I put her down, she'd shake herself and give herself a few licks to smooth her ruffled fur, then placidly saunter off.

What would my life be like if I could submit to God the way Zoe submits to me? How often does God lovingly ask,

*What're you gonna do about it?* as I struggle with worries and concerns that would be better left to His care?

These days, when confronted by a problem or unpleasant situation, I've tried to develop a habit of saying to God, "I can't *wait* to see what You're gonna do about it!" and then prayerfully handing it over to Him, confident He hears and cares. It's not always easy to simply go limp and let God take over, but if Zoe can learn to do that with me, I can learn to do it with my heavenly Father, knowing I'm safe in His arms.

*Marianne Campbell*

***Everything that's going on right now I'm giving to You, Lord. What else am I gonna do about it?***

# Courage and Compassion

*When he saw the crowds, he had compassion on them because they were confused and helpless, like sheep without a shepherd.*

—MATTHEW 9:36 (NLT)

He was a stray cat, a long-haired tuxedo with a Charlie Chaplin mustache. I had been feeding him for weeks, setting out kibble on my front porch, and I made a box to keep him dry during the drenching Oregon rains. I hoped to lure him into my home for a better life, but he always ran if I tried to touch him. Then I didn't see him for a week, until one morning, there he was when I opened my front door.

Unseasonably wet weather had dumped more than an inch of rain, leaving everything soggy. I gasped. Outside my door, poor Charlie lay in a puddle of water. I scooped him up and drove like a madwoman to the vet, who diagnosed a urinary blockage. He asked if I was willing to save a throwaway cat that might never be tamed. I agreed, not caring about the cost. All I could see were the kitty's pleading eyes.

I was reminded of the time, not long before, when I'd had to rush for help when my child overdosed on drugs. The doctor told me, "Insurance won't cover a suicide attempt." Was I prepared to face financial ruin to save my child? Yes—I would do whatever I could, no matter the cost.

In both cases, the question went far beyond money. I faced my own helplessness. I might not be able to rescue my child or a stray kitty. Should I try anyway? Of course. Love and compassion meant doing whatever I could to help.

Charlie Chaplin never became tame, but he always showed up for kibble. My child still battles addiction. Yet God gave me both the compassion and the longing to try to help. The cat struggled with urinary troubles and my precious child with addiction, but all of us—including those who might be seen as "throwaway" by some—are precious in His sight.

*Linda S. Clare*

***Lord, may compassion and love rule my heart,
and may I always be open to help all
Your creatures in their time of need. Amen.***

# Prayer Is Never Wasted

### *Pray without ceasing.*

–1 THESSALONIANS 5:17 (ESV)

For years, I'd heard that drinking eight glasses of water a day would be good for my health, so I felt pretty noble when I finally made it my New Year's resolution.

But as I walked into the kitchen one night, I was stunned to see my cat washing his face by scooping water out of my glass, dashing it on his face and circling his wet face with his paw. His bowl of water went untouched.

*Just how long has he been doing this? Could I have caught some cat disease?* I raced to the phone to call my vet, praying, *Please, God, let her answer right away. I could be seriously ill right now!*

She answered on the first ring—*Thank You, God.* "What's wrong with your cat?" she asked.

"Oh, it's not about Junior," I said. "It's about me. I just discovered that he has been scooping out water from my drinking glass to wash his face. What should I do?"

There was a moment's pause and then she said, "Keep your water in the refrigerator." I could swear I heard her chuckle as she hung up the phone.

"What a waste of time and worry," I said to the vet when she was examining Junior during his next regular checkup.

"But not a waste of prayer," she commented. "Prayer is never wasted." I've thought about what she'd said many times since then. Though it was something silly, that odd situation had led me to pray. If only I could stay as connected to God all the time. Now there's a subject for a resolution.

*Linda Neukrug*

**God, may I be inspired to pray more often, over big matters and small, so that I may become closer to You.**

# Lucky

*As a shepherd looks after his scattered flock when he is with them, so will I look after my sheep. I will rescue them from all the places where they were scattered on a day of clouds and darkness.*

—EZEKIEL 34:12 (NIV)

My brother Dave was an electrical lineman working a job in Nogales, Arizona, a busy hub for produce coming into the States from Mexico. One day, his job brought him in contact with lots of big trucks arriving with their deliveries. As he walked across a lot, he spotted a tiny tiger-striped kitten cowering and immobilized by fear as the monster vehicles lumbered around it.

Dave stooped to pick up the little bundle, wondering why it wasn't scurrying for cover on its own. When he looked at it more closely, he saw that the kitten had something wrong with its eyes and could not have navigated its way to safety if it had tried.

A trip to the vet confirmed a bad case of conjunctivitis. This is very dangerous for cats and, if left untreated, can lead to eye damage, blindness, and even death. The vet's first suggestion was that this cat should be put down because it would be too much work to nurse it back to health. He wasn't serious, of course, for he knew Dave and was familiar with the tender heart that lived inside the tall, dusty lineman. After dispensing the needed medication, he encouraged Dave to find a home for the kitten (knowing full well this one would likely end up joining the other cats, dogs, and horses that were cherished by Dave's family). Lucky had found a new home.

There have been times in my life when I have been immobilized—by blindness, illness, or fear. And each of those times, God has sent just the right person, Jesus with skin on, to set me on the right path again.

*Liz Kimmel*

***Father, thank You that You never leave me stranded and alone. I may feel lost, but You know where I am; You see and direct me to a place of safety. Amen.***

When you love a cat,
you are chosen, over and
over again, each day,
for a lifetime.

M. H. CLARK, POET AND WRITER

# Just to Know You're There

*"But while he was still a long way off, his father saw him and was filled with compassion for him; he ran to his son, threw his arms around him and kissed him."*

—LUKE 15:20 (NIV)

Twitch the cat is a feline's feline. Alternately moody and playful, aloof and cuddly, he maintains a diurnal schedule and keeps his own counsel. By day, he patrols the yard, ever on the lookout for trespassing rodents or usurping dogs. Other times, he keeps his skills sharp, leaping from behind the sofa or laundry basket to pounce on slippers or occasional bare toes.

One winter day, Twitch went out for a stroll and didn't return. The previous winter, he'd been gone for a spell and come home fatter than ever, smelling of wood smoke. I thought, *He's cuddled up by somebody else's fire, the dirty rat. He'll be back.*

A week went by, then another—and then a month. Several times a day, especially in the evening, I opened the door and called for him. Nothing. As the January temperatures reached their lowest point in years, I resigned myself to the worst.

Late one evening, passing the front door, I heard a faint mewing. I opened the door, and a skinny gray cat skittered across the threshold. I reached down to pet his matted coat and felt only bones. Half-starved, half-frozen, half-mad, Twitch had come home.

That evening, Twitch slept beside me. Neither of us slept much, as every little while, he woke me, crying for attention. Did he want more food? Water? Certainly not to go back outside. Petting him back to sleep, I understood what the poor thing truly needed: just to know that I was there.

I prayed, thanking God for watching over Twitch during that long month away—and watching over me always. Then Twitch and I went back to sleep.

*Lawrence W. Wilson*

***Thank You, Lord, for just being there.
No matter where I've been or what I've done,
You love me. How good that feels.***

# Lend a Helping ... Paw

***When Moses' hands grew tired, they took a stone and put it under him and he sat on it. Aaron and Hur held his hands up—one on one side, one on the other—so that his hands remained steady till sunset.***

—EXODUS 17:12 (NIV)

Although I've had dogs all my life, I'm a relatively new cat mama, having adopted bonded black tuxedo brothers named Dab and Hype about a year ago. They have extremely independent personalities, and though they like hanging out in the room with me, they only enjoy cuddling or petting on their own terms.

I've recently taken up yoga exercises, because the older I get, the less I'm able to do even simple stretches. My body is one big knot. I've watched the YouTube videos with dog yoga and wasn't surprised when my miniature schnauzer Gabby crawled under my downward-facing dog pose to see what I was doing.

However, when I sat on the floor and attempted (emphasis on *attempted*) the seated twist pose, I groaned in exasperation. My body wasn't cooperating at *all*. Suddenly I felt a pair of feline paws on my back, gently pressing me the right direction. Hype had apparently decided Mama couldn't do the pose by herself, so he needed to lend a paw.

Often in my life, I face situations where I could really use a hand—or paw—and I know those around me feel the same. Jesus reached out to those who needed a helping hand. My experience with Hype prompted me to look around and see who I can help today.

*Deb Kastner*

***Heavenly Father, as I go through my day today, help me to be on the lookout for opportunities to lend a helping hand to my family, friends, and neighbors. Amen.***

# The Good Gift

*Every good gift and every perfect gift is from above, coming down from the Father of lights, with whom there is no variation or shadow due to change.*

—JAMES 1:17 (ESV)

When we first met, I didn't know he was my gift. During a trip to the pet-supplies store before Christmas, I avoided the cages along the wall that held cats from a local shelter. I didn't want to be tempted to adopt another cat when I knew my family only wanted the one feline we already had.

But something drew my gaze to the cages from afar, and I spotted a cat with long white fur and a silver plume tail. He saw me too. His gaze locked with mine, and he wouldn't let me look away. As I moved closer to see the unusual cat, he still held my gaze. Then he opened his mouth slightly and emitted an adorable, deep meow that sounded like a plea to my heart. When I spoke with employees about him, they couldn't believe he hadn't been adopted yet, since he was gorgeous and had a friendly personality. We all expected he would be adopted before Christmas.

I prayed for the cat over Christmas, hoping he'd found a wonderful home. When I returned to the store around two weeks later, I checked the cages. The same white and silver cat met my gaze. And he gave me another unique meow, as if asking me to take him home.

Even my reluctant family couldn't deny the hand of Providence in keeping this cat for me. There was no other reason such a stunning and sweet cat wouldn't have been adopted yet. I was awed by God's kindness to me and this feline. And I understood for the first time how much God loves to give good gifts to His children. For on the Twelfth Day of Christmas that year, I adopted that cat—my special Christmas gift from God Himself.

*Jerusha Agen*

**Thank You for all the good gifts You have given me. Help me recognize the ones that are coming in the future—and give me the patience to wait when I need to.**

# Words Like Honey

***How sweet are your words to my taste,***
***sweeter than honey to my mouth!***
—PSALM 119:103 (NIV)

When the phone rings at the end of the workday, I know who it is before I even see the caller ID. My son is driving home from his job, a few hundred miles away, just checking in. His voice accompanies me around the kitchen as I clatter the cat-food dishes. It's feeding time.

The kittens have never met my son in person. They arrived as nearly new littermates a few weeks after his last visit home, adopted from the local animal shelter where they arrived from out of state, these tiny bundles of rescued love and fur. They have never met him, but whenever I put my son on speakerphone, they abandon their food and run to the sound of his voice. I cannot say for sure what so excites them: whether the vibrations of the phone remind them of their mother's purring or they are infected by my delight at hearing from him. Perhaps they recognize some family resemblance in his voice. But whatever the reason, they leap up onto the counter and chew on the corner of my phone case, trying to extract him, tasting his words.

I remember how God gave Ezekiel the scroll full of words, full of the Word of God, to eat and to speak, and it tasted sweet, like honey (Ezekiel 3:3). I recall how Jesus at His hungriest said that "Man shall not live on bread alone, but on every word that comes from the mouth of God" (Matthew 4:4, NIV).

Although I hope that the kittens do not actually end up eating my phone, they could certainly teach me something about devotion, this pair who love the voice and devour the words of a young man whom they have never met embodied with an affection that is pure and ravenous.

*Rosalind C. Hughes*

**O God, teach me to savor Your Word. Give me an appetite for the sweetness of Your grace and mercy. Fill me with the joy of Your unseen, unspeakable presence. Amen.**

# Up a Tree

***The LORD is with me; I will not be afraid.***
***What can mere mortals do to me?***

—PSALM 118:6 (NIV)

There was hard rain and strong wind last night, and the morning light revealed that a tree had come down, smashing through my fence. I gathered up my tools and walked out back to repair the damage. Passing an old sugar maple, I spied my neighbor's cat, a gray tabby, up in the branches. She's a cute little girl, always hanging around our back porch, looking for a handout or some scratches behind her soft ears. I watched as she tried to descend headfirst, then tail first, but every attempt ended in failure. She was stuck up there.

A firefighter friend of mine told me that the fire department really does receive calls about cats stuck up a tree. I asked, "What do you say to people when they call about a cat?" He said, "We tell them that nobody ever found a cat skeleton up a tree. Sooner or later, they always get down."

The problems I face—great and small—have me up a tree. But the situation is never hopeless. "Things are never as bad as they seem," said Miss Maudie in Harper Lee's *To Kill a Mockingbird*. The darkest nights always end in dawn, and the worst storms eventually blow themselves out. No matter how dark the room is, there is always a door. This is not a prescription for becoming passive and apathetic but for the honest recognition that I live out my life in the palm of God's hand and that nothing is going to happen to me that I can't handle with His help.

At day's end, with sore muscles and a repaired fence, I passed the maple tree again. The cat was gone. Somehow, some way, by God's grace, we always get down. After all, nobody ever found a cat skeleton up a tree.

*Louis Lotz*

***Lord, when I somehow manage to get myself up a tree, please help me see the way to get down again.***

# Getting Past My Gripping Anger

***But he walked right through the crowd
and went on his way.***

—LUKE 4:30 (NIV)

On the day I got the excellent report from my doctor that my cancer was gone, I phoned several friends, sharing the good news about my healing. But one friend acted as if he didn't care. I hung up after our conversation, depleted, betrayed, and angry. Suddenly, I felt myself adrift—even from Jesus.

Just then, my cat Hannah walked across the room. Following her was her brother, Rudy—puffed up like "two-ton Rudy" about to overtake her. And what did Hannah do? She acted annoyed but didn't stop. Instead, she kept walking, moving away from the scene of a potential fight. Her act of walking away was more potent than succumbing to a fierce battle with her brother would have been.

I found myself wanting to be as unflappable as Hannah, to get past my anger, to keep walking. To do that, I knew I had to forgive my friend and turn it over to God. Only then could I break this debilitating bondage of unforgiveness. I lowered my head and prayed for my friend. By laying my hurt and anger at the Lord's feet, I immediately felt lighter. I am sure that Hannah was a role model placed in front of me by Jesus to show me how to let go through forgiveness. Forgiving my friend who had offended me allowed me to walk unchained from his toxicity. I was as free as my cat Hannah, who was now snuggled with her brother, Rudy.

    I hugged Hannah and rewarded her with her favorite dish, sardines, along with a big silent thanks for modeling forgiveness. My Hannah helped me get my mind back on Jesus . . . by whose power I could move through any rough patch that threatened to overtake me.

*Terry Clifton*

***Thank You, Lord, for sending me models of how to move past anger and draw closer to You.***

# Milo the Rescue

*"The thief comes only to steal and kill and destroy; I have come that they may have life, and have it to the full."*

—JOHN 10:10 (NIV)

I brush my rescue cat, Milo, and I'm not sure which of us enjoys it more. Bringing his luxuriant fur to a sleek shine, as his paws knead the air, makes me smile. His trust is complete, and his peace is contagious.

We first rescued this black and white tuxedo cat as a kitten, scrawny as the stuffed mice he now plays with. But at the farm where he'd been born, he couldn't keep his paws off the chickens, which is why he had to go.

To see Milo today, you might question the validity of the hen-chasing stories. I've yet to see him hunt for anything but food dishes and patches of sunlight to flop in. This furball is the happiest creature I've ever met. He purrs even in his slumber. When he spots me across the room, he'll blink his eyes slowly as if to say, "I love you."

Milo appreciates his life, and his gratefulness is lavish. If this cat had a human twin, it would be me. As a teenager, I couldn't stay out of trouble. My lips and hands remained sticky with forbidden fruit, and no amount of washing removed the stain—or the hunger for more. But just as we rescued Milo, Jesus rescued me. He pulled me from the dangerous existence I'd chosen and gave me sanctuary in Him. The emptiness of my early life amplifies the abundance of the one I now lead. Grateful, I can rest in His peace. I've found my spot in the Son. My hunt is done.

*Heidi Gaul*

***Today, Lord, I'll take the time to meditate on gratitude in my own patch of sunlight. Thank You for the love You've shown to me. I love You, too.***

# His Faithful Provision

*Taste and see that the LORD is good; blessed is
the one who takes refuge in him.*

—PSALM 34:8 (NIV)

It was the day before Thanksgiving. I should have been grocery shopping, but here I was at the pet adoption shelter. I was reading a handwritten note attached to a cage—*abandoned female kitten, rescued from street.* A pair of soft, hazel-green eyes drew me to the furry bundle. I really wanted to adopt her. "Now, Sandra," I scolded myself, "your budget is *already* too tight."

As I walked from the shelter, a memory surfaced. I was a young girl, celebrating Thanksgiving on my grandparents' farm. Besides me, my mom, and my two sisters, there were six uncles, four aunts, and their numerous offspring. Grandpa and Grandma never had much money to raise their family. Added to that, Grandpa often took in abandoned animals dumped on the side of the road.

On that Thanksgiving Day, we sat at long folding tables overloaded with family contributions of mashed potatoes and gravy, turkey with all the trimmings, and an abundant variety of sweet delicacies. During Grandpa's lengthy prayer, I opened one eye to see a stray dog wander in and hide under a table.

Aunt Mildred dropped her napkin. As she bent under the table to retrieve it, she screamed—sending the family jumping back, with tables overturning, food flying.

Grandpa rushed to the intruder, but instead of shooing him away, Grandpa welcomed the hungry dog to the family. He announced with love, "Thanksgiving Day is the perfect day to thank the Lord that He is faithful to provide to *all* of us, in *all* ways."

I was back from my memory. Inspired by Grandpa and the long-ago four-legged Thanksgiving day guest, I turned around and rushed back to the shelter. This Thanksgiving, I would be holding a new purring family member in my arms as I thanked the Lord for His faithful provision.

*Sandra Clifton*

***It's not just Thanksgiving day, but every day, Lord, that we should share Your abundance with others. Thank You for Your generosity.***

# A Sunny Outlook

*I have learned how to be content with whatever I have. I know how to live on almost nothing or with everything. I have learned the secret of living in every situation. . . . For I can do everything through Christ, who gives me strength.*

—PHILIPPIANS 4:11–13 (NLT)

The stray kitty, a beautiful calico, appeared on my street, hungry and expecting. Since childhood, I've wanted to take in every animal I found, but this time, I couldn't handle any more due to my recovery from major shoulder surgery. Thankfully, my neighbor took in Mama Kitty, who soon gave birth to four wiggly kittens.

The litter included two more calico females, a tuxedo male, and a rare calico male. I was struggling to manage postoperative pain and faced possible permanent disability as a result. But each time I watched the kitties chase one another around our quiet street, I had to smile.

Suddenly, the male calico went missing. Weeks later, when I saw him again, he was missing a back leg. My neighbor, such a sweet soul, explained through tears that the now-teenage kitten had survived an accident that may have cost him his leg but didn't slow him down one bit. I thanked her for saving the little guy. "I've named him Sunny," she said. The cat promptly raced circles around our legs.

Sunny doesn't seem to care that he's a leg short or that it's unfair. His exuberant take on life reminds me that although I haven't been miraculously delivered out of my troubles, I don't have to adopt an attitude of doom and gloom. Sunny teaches me that I can choose to do the best I can with what I've got. Even in the tough times, I can flash the world a "Sunny" smile.

*Linda S. Clare*

**God, give me an outlook that finds contentment and peace in every situation, every day, rain or shine. Amen.**

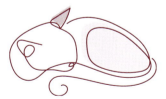

# Misha Loves Freedom

*It is for freedom that Christ has set us free.*
*Stand firm, then, and do not let yourselves be*
*burdened again by a yoke of slavery.*
—GALATIANS 5:1 (NIV)

I found Misha, a tiny, soaked, bedraggled kitten, in the rain outside my bank when I went there to make a night deposit. I have no idea how she had gotten there, nor where she'd come from. And then, after I took her in and gave her a home, she ran out of the vacation cabin I had rented when the door blew open, and she was lost for three weeks. I didn't think I would get her back.

Knowing her penchant for wandering, I have stopped trying to keep Misha from running outside; she loves her freedom outdoors. She is miserable when she is allowed to watch nature only from behind a window.

Misha wants to experience life at its fullest; she's never happy to be a spectator. She wants to chase the birds and lie in the sunshine. She loves climbing in the igloo on the deck and listening to the rain in person, not closed away with muffled sound and no raindrops.

I, too, have been given a great big, beautiful world with all the freedom to drink it in. So many times, it is not others but my own busyness that imprisons me. I lock myself away in my schedules and social media so much that my experiences become limited at best. I'm watching life pass by through a small window, instead of getting out there to experience it directly. And sometimes I allow myself to be limited by what others think instead of remembering God's loving acceptance and living in the freedom He gives me.

Misha reminds me of myself in some ways. My life at its fullest is mine to choose—the moment I decide to unlock the prison doors of my own making.

*Devon O'Day*

**God, let me dance in the freedom You have given me and let me give no one the keys to keep me locked away. Amen.*

For so many of us, cats have
a special place in our lives.
With their affection, grace,
companionship and personality,
cats can give us great joy and,
in so many ways, they
can also teach us—and remind
us—of helpful truths.

NEIL SOMERVILLE, AUTHOR

# Seventy-Seven and (Not) Counting

*"Lord, how often will my brother sin against me, and I forgive him? As many as seven times?" Jesus said to him, "I do not say to you seven times, but seventy-seven times."*

—MATTHEW 18:21–22 (ESV)

My seven-pound calico cat, Videa, emerged from the safety of the living room to approach my Great Pyrenees, Marshmallow—a giant, fluffy puppy of 130 pounds. She meowed softly and looked up at his face as she rubbed against his leg, asking him to "pet" her by smelling her back.

I shook my head at her relentless friendliness. Moments before, Marshmallow had scared her away when he had playfully stomped his front feet down right by her. He often made a game of stomping near my two cats or chasing them. I prevented such behavior whenever I could, but he was dauntless, since he thought it was so fun to watch them run away.

That day, he'd been able to frighten Videa away before I could intervene. Only a few minutes later, I was still angry about his behavior when Videa returned, eager to be friends with the fluffy beast. How could she have forgiven him so fast?

I shouldn't have been surprised. Though cats have a reputation of holding grudges, Videa had shown the most forgiving spirit I'd ever witnessed during the course of two puppies and their shenanigans. I'm sure she forgave my young dogs more than seventy-seven times.

When I watched her demonstrate forgiveness to Marshmallow yet again, I had to acknowledge the reason I was surprised—because I struggle to forgive so quickly and completely myself. How did Videa manage such forgiveness, even for the same repeated offense?

I realized the answer lay in the other characteristic Videa displayed: love. She could forgive so well because she loved so well. Thanks to her example, the next time I'm struggling to forgive someone, I'm going to focus on loving them the way the Lord wants me to. Then forgiveness will happen too.

*Jerusha Agen*

***Father, let my eagerness to love and forgive never waver in light of Your unending love and forgiveness for me. Amen.***

# Never Alone

***For He Himself has said, "I will never
leave you nor forsake you."***

—HEBREWS 13:5 (NKJV)

Every summer, I manage to catch at least one twenty-four-hour stomach bug that leaves me hunched over the porcelain bowl in misery.

This last time, the flu hit me just as I was about to go to bed that night. My husband was already asleep. I didn't want to bother him, so I braced myself for a very lonely, miserable night.

I lay curled up in a ball, sweat slicked from my fever, as my stomach rumbled and complained. Finally, I could wait no longer and stumbled to the bathroom. No sooner had I dropped to my knees than my fiercely independent tuxedo black cat Dab appeared next to me, one paw on the toilet rim and the other on my back. He quite literally "talked" me through the episode with his patient meows.

And it didn't happen just once, either. Dab was my sick buddy throughout the night, every single time I ran to hunch over the toilet. This cat, who refuses to be petted except on his terms and will throw a conniption fit if someone tries to pick him up, gently accompanied me through the dark night.

King David had many such dark nights (minus the flu) and often wrote about them in his psalms. I think we've all had our share, and no doubt there will be more to come. How comforting it is to know we have a God who never leaves or forsakes us. No matter what today will hold, I can count on the Lord to be with me.

*Deb Kastner*

***Thank You, Lord, for being with me through my dark nights and for sending Your helpers to sit with me.***

# The Perfect Mouser

***Blessed be the Lord, who daily loads us with benefits, the God of our salvation! Selah.***
−PSALM 68:19 (NKJV)

**"I** have mice!" Robin's face pulled into a grimace of disgust. "I don't know what to do. I've put out traps and tried everything. They've invaded the cushions on my back porch. I've lost my favorite quiet-time spot."

"The cat eats mine," I said nonchalantly, not processing the fact that I don't own a cat.

"What cat? I thought you were allergic to cats."

"Oh, he's not my cat."

Robin's brow furrowed, and she was right to be confused. I *am* allergic, and I don't own a cat. But I do have a cat that lives in my bushes. He's mangy and missing one ear and completely feral, stalking like a lion outside my house as if he owns the place. His favorite hobby is dropping little mice at my front doorstep.

I've never thought much about "Not My Cat." I've certainly never thought to be grateful. But as I heard my friend's woes, I changed my perspective on my competent, low-maintenance mouser friend who has adopted my family. He daily loads us with benefits, and I'd never thanked him once. In truth, I'd felt nothing but disgust for his little "presents."

As I drove away from my friend, I couldn't help thinking about how many times God has done this exact thing for me. He hides in the bushes of my life, taking care of me in ways I don't even know to be grateful for, providing, caring, guarding my life with His love. I wish I knew how to thank Not My Cat. Because of my allergies, he really is the perfect cat for my family. Instead, I'll thank my heavenly Father for knowing what I need before I need it. I think He and Not My Cat are in on it together.

*Tracy Joy Jones*

***Thank You for all the blessings You send that I don't recognize. I'm grateful that You pay such close attention to my needs.***

# "Shouldn't We Pray?"

***The earnest prayer of a righteous person has great
power and produces wonderful results.***

—JAMES 5:16 (NLT)

Gray was missing. To someone else, the disappearance of a stray cat who'd showed up one day and left a few weeks later may not have meant anything. And to my grandfather, a lifelong cat hater, it should have represented that, but it didn't. Over the years, Pop had owned dogs, all cared for with gentleness and love. Cats were ignored and certainly not allowed into his home or heart.

But a thin gray cat showed up outside and adopted my grandfather as its own. We would watch the cat weave around Pop's legs when he walked out to the mailbox. We saw it curl up next to him as he worked in his toolshed. We saw this busy man reach down to gently pat the animal and smile. The cat had worked its way into Pop's heart. Discussions began about allowing it inside the house.

However, one day when Pop opened the door to go out, Gray, as he'd named the cat, wasn't lying on the deck. All day, Pop watched for the cat, wondering where it had gone. Over the next weeks, we saw him mourn the loss of his tiny companion. We talked about it in hushed tones when our young daughters and I came to visit. Our four-year-old spoke with the faith of a child.

"Shouldn't we pray?"

Knowing the cat was probably gone forever, as well as not wanting to harm the tenuous threads of a child's faith, I hesitated for a moment. But she was determined, so we prayed for the cat to return. And the end of the story? The next day, Gray was back, purring against Pop's legs. And I experienced a child's faith in action.

*Cathy Mayfield*

**God, what else is possible that I didn't believe could be so? I'm praying with the faith of a child.**

# Overflow

***This I say for your own profit, not that I may put a leash on you, but for what is proper, and that you may serve the Lord without distraction.***
—1 CORINTHIANS 7:35 (NKJV)

My cat Kris likes to drink water from the bathroom sink, preferring the water be running, so he can lick it as it flows. I indulge him because he's the boss. One recent day, I ran the water for Kris before jumping in the shower. I washed my hair and sang a song or two, and when I stepped out, the water was two inches deep on the floor, a stream still flowing merrily from the sink. Had the cat inadvertently pushed down the stopper? Kris sat in the closet, momentarily safe from the encroaching flow. It took every towel I owned to mop the floor and sop up every drawer and shelf in the bathroom. I was disgusted with myself, but I had to admit, this mishap was a symptom of a bigger problem.

For days, I'd felt a vague sense of unease. My life didn't seem to be running as smoothly as it might. I'd been so busy caught up in the cares of the world that I'd neglected my time with the Lord. *Oh, Jesus, when I take my eyes off You, things just don't go right.*

Distractions, the bane of my existence. But I knew what I had to do to get my life in order. Each morning, before the world intruded, I needed to get back to spending time with Jesus. I needed to read the Bible, pray for those on my list, and talk to Him about my cares. I could do it!

*Pat Butler Dyson*

***Lord, when I start to think I'm too busy for You, I need a reminder of how much I need that time. Help me remember.***

# We All Knead Someone

*"Who of you by worrying can add a*
*single hour to your life?"*

—LUKE 12:25 (NIV)

As the clock struck twelve, revelers welcomed the New Year with neighborhood fireworks. In years past, my friend's German shepherd, Khalisah, had suffered from severe anxiety. Thunder had always triggered extreme fear, and holidays with noisy sound effects left the dog cowering in a corner, whimpering, with her tail between her legs.

But this year, a stray cat had adopted Khalisah's family. Nigel Thornberry, a black male kitty, had quickly settled into the household.

Khalisah's "mom" had worried about the upcoming New Year's Eve fireworks. She couldn't bear the thought of her poor dog's trauma during all the loud noise. All she could do was try to keep Khalisah feeling safe next to her on the sofa.

When the booms, bangs, and whistles began, Khalisah whined in fear. But before my friend could even comfort the dog, Nigel jumped onto the sofa and went to work massaging Khalisah's fur as only a cat can. Nigel kneaded Khalisah's back, and the dog stopped whimpering. Before long, Khalisah put her head down to enjoy Nigel's comforting massage. Khalisah's mom was amazed.

But Nigel didn't stop there. No matter what day of the year, if thunder or fireworks crash and boom, Nigel rushes to Khalisah's side and begins "making biscuits." Khalisah relaxes, and after a bit more comforting, Nigel curls up beside his doggie friend.

Most of us have experienced some degree of trauma. A sound or even a smell can trigger bad memories. Nigel Thornberry teaches me to lean on God and hang on to my own fur babies when I am fearful. Just by petting my cat, I lower my own anxiety. If I'm really blessed, my cat will crawl onto my lap and make biscuits. Like Khalisah, I'm glad for the God-sent gift of kitties who seem to understand that everybody "kneads" somebody sometime.

*Linda S. Clare*

***God, even if I can't knead You, I will always need You.***

# Reassuring L.E.

*Comfort, oh comfort my people, says your God.*
—ISAIAH 40:1 (JPS)

Our cat L.E. is a talker and has an extensive vocabulary. She does have a normal meow and a soft purr, but she also yowls and howls, barks, warbles, chirps, squeaks, and makes a variety of different sounds for which my husband, Keith, and I make up words like *murfing*.

She is most definitely Keith's cat. When it's clear he's going to leave the house, she complains by "chittering." She stares at him until he looks her way, then she deliberately turns her back on him and goes on complaining, biting off her chitters with apparent annoyance that he would dare go off and leave her.

So when Keith was in the hospital, L.E. did not know how to behave. She was surprised when I came home without him again and again. She wandered from room to room, searching. Now and then she'd let out a sharp call, as if summoning him to her presence. When he didn't come, the call morphed into a piteous meow of loss.

I had to comfort L.E. "It'll be all right," I found myself telling her. "Keith is being taken care of. He'll be back home with us before you know it."

Soon it became evident to me that in the process of trying to convince the cat that there would be a good outcome, I was convinced as well. It was as if L.E. had decided that the only way I'd have faith in Keith's coming home was if she made me keep saying it over and over again. Or maybe it was God speaking through a very vocal feline.

*Rhoda Blecker*

***Thank You, God, for giving me ways to grow my faith and trust in You.***

# Millions of Cats

***Humble yourselves before the Lord,
and he will lift you up.***

—JAMES 4:10 (NIV)

I just finished rereading the children's classic *Millions of Cats* by Wanda Gág. This sweet book about an older couple in search of a new pet has captured my heart for decades.

In the story, the old man finds a hill covered with millions of cats. How can he pick just one when all of them are exquisite? He decides to let the cats choose among themselves which is prettiest. But each one believes he is, and a huge squabble ensues. When the dust settles, they've all disappeared, save for a single scrawny kitten. The reason? He didn't consider himself special, so the others left him alone. Through the love the old couple share with him, this little kitty truly becomes the most beautiful cat in the world.

I shut the book with a satisfied snap.

Like those millions of cats, I've wasted time competing to be the best, the most creative, the fastest. I've discovered that sort of contest is impossible—and pointless—to win.

Then I remember Jesus's humility and see beauty as it's meant to be.

As with the scraggly kitten in my storybook, there is nothing outstanding about me. When people look at me, they don't see a celebrity, a genius, or anyone special. But Jesus does. He seeks the treasure within me. To Him, I'm beautiful—the most beautiful me in the entire universe. And that's enough. Because like that little kitten in the book, I've found worth in His eyes, and my spirit flourishes under His care.

*Heidi Gaul*

***Lord, thank You for all the ways that You have lifted me up and made me feel special. I know that with You, I never have to feel as if I'm in a competition.***

# Speckles, Remain Calm!

***Cast all your anxiety on him because he cares for you.***
—1 PETER 5:7 (NIV)

Just as my tortoiseshell cat, Speckles, has multicolored fur, her personality is multifaceted too. When Speckles appeared as a stray, she was Miss Courteous Cat, meowing politely from the bushes until I invited her into her forever home. Speckles the Fearless Feline scampers up the tallest tree, arriving at the selected teeny branch, just to sharpen her claws. Speckles the Huntress patrols my property against all types of nonhuman critters.

A new and unexpected side of her personality revealed itself during her annual checkup at the veterinarian's office. Then she became Speckles the Scaredy Cat. In one of the exam rooms, she leaped onto a shelf of the tall cabinet, her wild eyes darting around the room, searching for an escape route amid all the unfamiliar territory. When Speckles sent out her loud distress yowl, the vet quickly arrived from a nearby room. No amount of soothing sounds or comforting hugs from me would calm my feline.

I shook my head in disbelief at Speckles's reaction. Then I realized I, too, react with anxiety in certain situations. My mother often told how she chased four-year-old me around the doctor's office so that the physician could administer my vaccine. Many years later I am still the Impatient Patient during my annual screening—minus the running around. Learning a new computer program or navigating busy city streets brings out my jitters. My calming routine is taking a deep breath and then whispering a personalized version of 1 Peter 5:7: *God, take all my anxieties, because I know You care for me.*

When Speckles and I return to the sounds and scents of her territory, she eases into her comfortable routine. For me, my soul seeks the familiar solitude of home. We are back to being the Tranquil Twosome.

*Glenda Ferguson*

***God, take all my anxieties, because
I know You care for me.***

# Tigre Forgives

*But if you do not forgive others their sins,*
*your Father will not forgive your sins.*

—MATTHEW 6:15 (NIV)

Tigre's mother was a feral that came to the farm and left her whole litter of kittens before they were weaned. She left them in a bucket by the barn, and Tigre was the only kitten to survive. Her will was incredibly strong. She grew into adulthood as a powerful rodent ridder on the farm but never allowed me to touch her. Because of that, I was unable to catch her to get her fixed. After being missed for a few weeks, she showed up pregnant and gave birth in the dog's igloo to four little kittens who looked just like her.

I was very worried she would not have good maternal skills because her mother had abandoned her. But she fed and cleaned those babies and even allowed me to pick them up when it was time to wean them. While she was afraid to trust me enough to let me touch her, she knew to trust I would not harm her babies. When she needed to let go and let them learn to be fed away from her, she knew I would step in with what they needed. She didn't abandon them because she was abandoned. She mothered them with all the care she was not given. She mothered with what she herself had needed.

I have heard many excuse their poor choices by blaming bad parental upbringing. We can't change how our childhoods began or who our parents were, but we can make good choices as adults. As I have learned to make better choices in my own life, I have found the grace to forgive those in my life who didn't have the strength to do so. Grace is a brave gift, and it changes the ripples in every pond it's allowed in.

*Devon O'Day*

**Father, do not let me continue to make bad choices because someone in my past made bad choices for me. Help me learn not only from my mistakes but from the mistakes of others—even those who hurt me. Amen.**

We can sometimes spend too much time flailing around, and fall deaf to the essentials of existence. And maybe this is what your cat is telling you with its stillness, its contemplation and benevolent attitude: "I am here, keeping watch over you and looking out for you. This too shall pass."

STÉPHANE GARNIER, AUTHOR

# Small Glimpses

*The wolf will live with the lamb, the leopard will lie down with the goat, the calf and the lion and the yearling together; and a little child will lead them.*
—ISAIAH 11:6 (NIV)

I arrived at Aunt Nell and Uncle Billy's house for a weekend stay. I placed my bags in the guest room, greeted my family, and went in search of their cat, Janie. I found her curled up on the stool at the end of the kitchen counter. She purred as I bent down to greet her and then stroked her black fur with white spots.

Janie has the distinction of being the one cat that hasn't caused my allergies to act up. I love cats, but their hair and dander tickle my nose, cause me to sneeze, and make my eyes turn red and itchy. Janie wasn't a special breed, but she was a special cat.

She often spent her days roaming the fields that surrounded my aunt and uncle's property in the country. When Janie was inside, I could usually find her napping on her favorite stool. That's the only place I ever saw cat hair in their home.

I didn't see Janie when I went to bed that night, but I awoke the next morning to the sound of her purring and a weight on my backside. With the turn of my head, I saw her curled up on the back of my legs. Janie meowed at my movements and then removed herself so I could sit up.

I scratched behind her ears and marveled at my ability to sleep with her and still breathe through my nose. I firmly believe God had a hand in this miracle. I am thankful for all the small glimpses God gives me now that reveal the wonder I'll find in my eternal home.

*Crystal Storms*

*God, thank You for small, everyday miracles, like the miracle of our breath and of hypoallergenic cats.*

# The Calico's Comfort

***May your unfailing love be my comfort,
according to your promise to your servant.***

—PSALM 119:76 (NIV)

The day I washed the small dog bed our puppy had outgrown, I had no idea what was about to happen. My intention was to put the bed in storage, but I made a fatal mistake. I removed it from the dryer and set it on a bench in the foyer.

I left the room, and when I returned later, the bed had been claimed by my calico cat, Videa. The bed would never belong to a dog again. Videa had fallen in love with the dog bed—it was perfect for a cat who loved plush softness and warmth.

I'd never seen Videa look so comfortable and adorable as she did on that bed. The kitty who normally had to curl up to keep warm could lie stretched on her side with her white belly fur exposed to the air.

But I soon became aware there was a downside to all that comfort. Videa barely left the bed. She fit in quick meals, but immediately returned to the comfort of the bed. She stopped playing with toys, which led to weight gain. Saddest of all, she didn't join me for our traditional lap time in the evenings.

As I wondered if I should limit Videa's access to the bed for her own good, I realized she might not be the only one who had gotten too comfortable. The more comfortable I became with my life, the less I wanted to leave the house, connect with people, or try new things. Worse, being comfortable led to complacency in my walk with the Lord. I spent less time in prayer and the Word, letting my relationship with God get out of shape. It turns out too much comfort can be a bad thing, unless I'm finding my comfort in Christ.

*Jerusha Agen*

***Lord, help me leave behind the comforts that do more harm than good, and to seek ultimate comfort in You.***

# One Nervous Kitty

***Be completely humble and gentle; be patient,
bearing with one another in love.***

—EPHESIANS 4:2 (NIV)

I opened the box and saw a gray-and-black tabby
staring up at me.

"Her name is Princess," my then-husband said proudly.

We'd had to give away our older cat because she didn't
appreciate our toddler's affection, so Daddy thought a
younger kitty would be a nice surprise. I thought so, too,
until I picked Princess up and she left a layer of cat hair
on my sweater. This was beyond normal shedding. When
I put her down, she took off down the hall and hid in the
bathroom. For three days. Anyone who went in to give
her some love came out covered in hair.

"She might need to go back," I whispered one night.

Then, while watching a movie with the kids, I saw
Princess sitting by the bathroom door. A few minutes
later, she'd inched closer. By the time the movie ended,
she was in the living room, allowing the boys to pet her.
She wasn't shedding as much. By the next day, she was a

member of the family. She'd just needed us to be patient with her while she adjusted.

Recently, I saw a photo of Princess on my computer. The son who'd been a toddler when his dad brought Princess home was ten years old in the picture, snuggling with Princess on his bunk bed. If we'd returned Princess to the shelter over a little anxiety and extra cat hair, we would have missed out on a sweet pet.

I wondered what other friendships I had given up on too quickly? How often did I mistake shyness or awkward behavior for *She must not like me* or *We could never be friends*? Memories of Princess's transition into our home motivate me to approach each new relationship with Christlike patience.

*Jeanette Hanscome*

***Help me recognize the times when I'm not giving others enough of a chance, Lord. And if I'm being a nervous kitty myself, please encourage others to be patient with me.***

# Call Security

*"But whoever listens to me will live in safety and be at ease, without fear of harm."*

—PROVERBS 1:33 (NIV)

**M**y wife, Sandra, and I returned home late one night from a visit with neighbors. As I entered the kitchen from the garage, I distinctly heard the sound of a toilet flushing. Sandra gasped. "Someone's in the house," she said, stifling a scream. I gestured for her to return to the garage. Wanting to stay close to me, she shook her head, signaling no, as she turned me around toward the bathroom. We looked like Lucy and Ricky in the episode where they move to the country and presume there is a break-in. As we crept past our front door, I grabbed an umbrella from the coat-tree. *Oh, mighty warrior*, I thought.

All my stubborn excuses for ignoring endless mailers, phone calls, and text messages with offers from home security companies rapidly passed through my adrenaline-pumped mind: *They're just trying to scare us to make money. We live in a safe neighborhood. Our home has little street traffic. Why would we need an elaborate security system?*

We warily approached the main bath with umbrella in hand, ready for battle. The door was open a crack. The light was on. I kicked the door open, stepped back, and beheld our fat gray cat, Sammy, mounted on the tank of our new top-flush toilet. Upon seeing us, he meowed, stood up, and then sat down. And voilà—the sound of swirling water.

After our hearts slowed down and we stopped laughing, I realized the Lord had used Sammy to give me a gentle prod to take more seriously the safety of my family. I would check out our security options in the morning.

*Terry Clifton*

***Thank You, Lord, for Your grace, patience, and love. You forgive and correct us, even as we wrestle with our human frailty. Amen.***

# Fuzzy Faith

*So then you are no longer strangers and aliens,
but you are fellow citizens with the saints
and members of the household of God.*
—EPHESIANS 2:19 (ESV)

Fuzzy is one of the community cats that live in our neighborhood. The first time I saw her, she was chasing a mouse across the road. Her ribs showed through her patchy gray fur, and one ear was torn. Clearly, she lived by her wits and her claws. I watched for her each morning as I walked and tried to get close enough to pet her. She wasn't interested.

One day a thread on the neighborhood social-media page mentioned Fuzzy. Winter had arrived, and people were concerned. One woman put a heating pad set on "low" on her porch. Two others regularly set out food. As time passed, Fuzzy learned that the blessings of grateful dependence were far better than the imagined benefits of independence. Her fur grew in, and her wounds healed as she learned to trust the kind people reaching out to her.

In my young adult years, I was a lot like Fuzzy. I prided myself on independence and self-sufficiency—until my

**140**

willful decisions left me scarred and empty. I felt hungry for peace, joy, and relationships. In His mercy, God drew me into a church family that fed me with His Word and cared for me with His love. I grew spiritually healthy and learned to trust in God to provide everything I needed.

Every time I see Fuzzy I remember how gracious and compassionate my heavenly Father is. I thank Him for connecting me with kind, godly people and rescuing me from myself.

*Lori Hatcher*

***Lord, thank You for reaching out in Your compassion and healing my wounds. I know now that blessed dependence is the best way to live.***

# The Hiding Place

*You are my hiding place; you will protect me from trouble and surround me with songs of deliverance.*
—PSALM 32:7 (NIV)

I'd called and searched the house from top to bottom. For twenty-four hours I fretted, worried, and prayed. Still, my cat, Benny, was missing. As fear tightened its grip, I imagined all sorts of awful outcomes. Had my all-black "house panther" somehow escaped the house and been run over or catnapped? The worst picture of all was imagining life without my furry friend.

Benny and his twin brother, Toulouse-Lautrec, had purred at my side as I crammed for college finals. They'd romped over me at 3 a.m. as I tried to sleep. And when we lost Toulouse, Benny mourned alongside me. Benny even became "Best Cat" at my wedding. I couldn't lose him too.

"Benny! Benny-boo, Ben!" I tried calling every pet name I could remember: Benji-beans, Benny-licious, Ben-there-done-that. I threw in his full name, Benjamin Franklin Blackcat, so he'd know he was in trouble. Nothing. Close to tears, I sank down on the fireplace hearth next to some built-in bookcases and prayed again.

God seemed far away. Maybe finding my cat wasn't in the plan—or maybe God was just too busy to man the Lost & Found desk. Yet the longer I sat, the more I remembered all the times God's love had provided me a place of refuge and comfort. When I'd had to face difficulties, God's door was always open. Surely God loved animals as much as I did.

I steeled myself to accept the inevitable, but this time I felt reassured. Even if Benny never came back, I would always love him. And God would watch over both him and Toulouse. I stood . . . and something told me to look behind some dusty old books in the bookcase.

Out popped Benny with a *meowff?* as if he were saying, *What took you so long*? I hugged Benny hard and thanked God that I always have a hiding place in Him.

*Linda S. Clare*

***Thank You, Lord, for always being my comfort, my refuge, and a listening ear.***

# Simple Joy

*Though you have not seen him, you love him; and even though you do not see him now, you believe in him and are filled with an inexpressible and glorious joy.*

—1 PETER 1:8 (NIV)

The sun warms my body as I lounge on my favorite chaise. A gentle breeze stirs the air. Neighborhood sounds meld into calming white noise, and I smell a barbecue nearby. I reach for my glass and sip some iced tea.

Sprawled across my lap, my tuxedo cat, Milo, stretches his paws to knead the air. His adoring gaze never leaves my face. A loud purr rumbles against my ribs.

I haven't petted him or scratched his chin. I've done nothing aside from giving him a quiet place to rest. He's elated just to be here with me, sharing a few minutes together. Knowing this makes me smile.

I understand the simple joy Milo feels in my presence. Like him, I have a safe place to land when I need a break from the world's bustle. During the quiet time I spend alone with Jesus, the serenity I experience restores me. He need not *do* anything—the privilege of His presence is enough. I sense His love for me and am filled with deep, abiding joy.

My simple need for His company—along with my complete trust in Him—delight Jesus. As I smile at Milo, I suspect Jesus is smiling too.

He is peace. He is joy. He alone is enough.

*Heidi Gaul*

***I always feel safe when I'm in Your lap, Lord.
Thank You for always being there for me.***

# How Did You Respond?

*Therefore, as God's chosen people . . . clothe
yourselves with compassion, kindness,
humility, gentleness and patience.*

—COLOSSIANS 3:12 (NIV)

My mittened hands fumbled to open the latch of the barn door. I'd been outside only a few moments, but already my cheeks ached from the cold, which matched my heart—way below zero. I'd run into an acquaintance who had a reputation for being difficult. She snarled at me when I said hello. *Next time I see her, I'm going to totally ignore her!* I thought.

I swung open the barn doors. The light from my headlamp cast its beam as I loaded the sled with flakes of alfalfa for the horses. Two eyes glowed from the top of the stack. A skinny tortoiseshell cat sat huddled in a ball, trying to keep warm. As soon as the light danced across it, it scooted backward to hide. "Aw, kitty, did somebody dump you out here? I bet you're hungry." The gold slits of its eyes glared at me.

After feeding the horses, I went into the house and filled a bowl with cat food. My heart felt warm from the

146

kindness I would offer. But as soon as I stretched on my toes to set the bowl on the hay, the cat swatted my hand and disappeared. I chuckled at its antics.

I heard a still small voice: *That's not how you responded to your acquaintance.* My spirit grieved as I realized what I'd done. I couldn't control how others acted, but I could control what I did.

A couple of days later I smiled when I greeted the woman. It didn't matter that she only nodded in return.

*Rebecca Ondov*

***Lord, help me to walk in Your example
of kindness. Amen.***

# **Known and Loved**

***The LORD is good, a refuge in times of trouble.***
***He cares for those who trust in him.***
—NAHUM 1:7 (NIV)

Last winter, my cat, Tigger, started acting strangely. When I tried to rub his favorite spot behind his ears, he pulled away and meowed. He stared into my eyes and meowed loudly. He was usually a quiet cat, so I knew he was trying to tell me something. Despite having no other symptoms of being ill, his odd behavior convinced me that something was wrong. My husband thought it was silly to take a cat to the vet simply because he was "acting weird," but I was convinced Tigger needed help. It's a good thing, because he was suffering from a urinary blockage, a life-threatening condition if it's not detected early enough. The vet cleared the blockage and put Tigger on a special diet, but he cautioned me that this problem often recurs.

A few days ago, Tigger climbed into my lap and meowed in my face, just as he had before. I was sure he had another blockage, which a trip to the vet confirmed.

My husband couldn't believe how easily I was able to interpret Tigger's behavior. "When you love someone, you know what's normal for them," I said. "You know their struggles, so it's easy to figure out when something's wrong. What's harder is knowing how to help them."

The next day, a friend accidentally hurt my feelings, but I pretended things were fine. My friend never knew that I was upset. But I can't hide my hurt or pretend with God. He reads my behavior even more easily than I can read Tigger's. As my heavenly Father, He knows everything about me. He knows when I'm upset and struggling with something. He knows my weaknesses, those recurring problems that are always there, even when I try to pretend I'm fine. Insecurity. Fear. Self-doubt. I can't hide it from Him.

God already knows my struggles, but climbing up into His lap to tell Him about it never fails to comfort me. And best of all, He always knows how to help.

*Diane Stark*

***God, thank You for knowing me inside and out. Amen.***

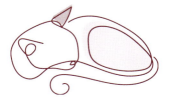

# A Gift

***Love never fails.***
−1 CORINTHIANS 13:8 (NKJV)

My husband, Terry, and I wandered the aisles of our local no-kill animal shelter. The unexpected loss of our sweet cat Barbara the previous month had left a gaping hole of grief in me. I was not looking to replace her but to give a young cat a better life. I spotted a set of doleful eyes surveying me from behind a cardboard box. I tried to coax the kitten to me. I cooed and whispered to her. She didn't budge, just intensely stared at me.

A teenage volunteer appeared at my side. "This one had a rough start. They found her abandoned in an alley. We have more lively kittens down this aisle."

I followed the girl. There were so many cats and kittens needing to be adopted. But I kept circling back to the little one with the piercing green eyes. Her eyes spoke fear but also cried for someone to love her.

I turned to my husband and declared, "This is the one! She needs love as much as I need to give it."

As soon as our new kitten, Hannah, got home, she disappeared under the bed. Several days went by, and no coaxing, baby talk, or proffered food brought her out of her hidey-hole.

About the same time, I was bedridden with a severe case of the flu. As I wearily fell asleep one night, I pondered, *Lord, did I make a mistake bringing a new kitten into this house*? As sunrise approached, a deep guttural purring in my ear and a rhythmic digging into my shoulder awakened me. Hannah had somehow instinctively recognized that at that moment, I needed attention as much as she did.

Hannah, no longer the hiding and fearful kitty, and I formed a love bond that morning that only the Lord could create. Love never fails because God is in it.

*Sandra Clifton*

***Lord, are you looking to create a love bond in my life? Lead the way.***

Cats are open to opportunity. Their spontaneous outlook makes the world a place of wonder and adventure.

ALISON DAVIES, WRITER

# Charlie "No Tail"

***A gentle answer turns away wrath,***
***but a harsh word stirs up anger.***

—PROVERBS 15:1 (NIV)

Charlie was a beautiful Siamese cat I saw on a Facebook page placing unwanted, lost, or found animals. His finder was a young mother who saw Charlie in her neighborhood and took him in. He had some intestinal issues that she was unable to take on financially, so she re-homed him with me.

I soon found that Charlie had a superpower—an uncanny ability to calm the beast in everyone. His beautiful blue eyes would look into mine and instantly put me at ease. He would "pet" the beard of our farmhand, Joe, and purr so loudly you could hear him from across the room. We have no idea why his tail was only two inches long, but we all agreed it wasn't from a fight. Because even my surliest old barn cats who hated everything and everyone would bound up to Charlie, ready to hiss and scratch, only to stop short after looking into his sweet face. They would walk away calmly with no angst or agitation.

It occurred to me that Charlie soothed an agitated soul by quietly stopping, without fear, and meeting the onslaught of aggression by sitting down and letting the anger fly over and around him. It diffused the situation. Every. Single. Time. He didn't try to defend himself. He didn't run. He just let the steam blow, and it took the wind from anger's sails and left the territory defenders walking away in total acceptance that Charlie was OK.

Charlie has taught me that when someone is coming at me with irrational anger or angst, it's never about me. It's 100 percent always about them. When we let the storm happen without becoming a storm in response, the outcome is usually totally different. A scream for a scream or insult for insult is not the answer. But a gentle attitude and kind word not only changes the direction of the storm but often calms the waves altogether and settles the wind into soft breezes.

*Devon O'Day*

***Today I'm going to step back, Lord, and use a gentle reaction instead. I'll trust You to handle any battles that need to be fought.***

# Time to Trust

***Fear not: for I am with thee.***

—ISAIAH 43:5 (KJV)

Gracie, the two-pound abandoned kitten I found at our back steps four years ago, is making progress overcoming her fears. She's even begun, on special occasions, to purr.

I'd stopped taking her to the veterinarian because of her terror. Because she's an inside cat, my vet reluctantly agreed. But the problem of trimming her nails remained. Somehow Gracie knew when I was about to do it and hid—often avoiding me all day. Or else we'd struggle together, and maybe I'd get two nails trimmed.

One day, I sat down by her on our favorite chair. Usually she vacates a chair if she can't have it all, but she stayed there and even purred and shut her green eyes. It was a lovely moment.

*Why not trim her nails now?* The tiny red-handled feline nail scissors lay within my reach. Rather than hold Gracie down, I laid the scissors by her paws. Startled, she sniffed them cautiously. I continued rubbing her gray head and whispered, "I'm going to trim your nails,

Grace Face." She reached out and touched the scissors with one apprehensive paw. Finally, she glared at me. "It's OK, Sweetie." I moved my hand down to one foot and massaged it tenderly. Her purring resumed as she shut her trusting eyes. Gently I exposed a couple of very long nails and snipped them quickly. No struggle! *Snip, snip, snip* . . . In less than a minute, both front paws were properly trimmed. Her sandpaper-like pink tongue licked my hand.

*Marion Bond West*

***Lord, enable me to trust like Gracie when there's something you must prune from my life.***

# Zoe Needs Help

***God is our refuge and strength,***
***an ever-present help in trouble.***

—PSALM 46:1 (NIV)

Our cat, Zoe, trotted into the bedroom and prepared to leap up on the bed for her afternoon nap. As she'd done thousands of times before, she sized up the height of the bed and the distance of her jump.

Then with dainty steps, she positioned herself for the spring. Splat! She ended up clinging ungracefully to the edge of the bed. Poor Zoe. At fourteen years old, she wasn't a kitten anymore, and her legs simply didn't have the strength they once had. She seemed embarrassed or maybe discouraged, and she slid down the side of the bed, claws skipping over the coverlet, and began to slink away.

"Aw, poor kitty," I said, picking her up. "You're not as spry as you used to be, but you're still my precious puss." Then I gently placed her on the bed and scratched her behind the ears until she purred.

As I pondered my aging pet, I thought, *This is just how God deals with me in my life.* All the times I go for something and come up short or completely miss, God is there to pick me up, comfort me, set me on the right path, and give me something to make me smile. In fact, what He gives me is always something better than what I was going for in the first place. He reminds me that He loves me in spite of my failures. When I am weak, He is strong and in control, the God who is able to raise me up.

Zoe wasn't thinking of me when she made her failed leap, but I was nearby and happy to help her, just as God, my Father in heaven, is also near to me and all believers, ready to help, ready to forgive, ready to save.

*Marianne Campbell*

***God, thank You for being near to me and picking me up when I slip.***

# A Beautiful Birthday Present

*I will sustain you and I will rescue you.*

—ISAIAH 46:4 (NIV)

"What do you want for your birthday?" my husband, Tony, asked.

I shrugged my shoulders and went back to searching the Internet for a used trumpet for our son Solomon. One link led to another, and soon I found myself staring at a blurry picture of a sickly looking white kitten and the words *Needs a Home.*

I've wanted a white kitten ever since I was ten years old and read about Snowdrop in the sequel to *Alice's Adventures in Wonderland, Through the Looking-Glass.* I called the number on the listing. An hour later Tony and I were on our way to pick up my birthday present, two counties away.

As we got closer to the destination, I worried about the way the kitten looked in the picture. "What if he's sick?" I asked. "Maybe this is a silly idea." With each passing mile, my fears grew deeper.

Finally, we were on the street and counting down the mailboxes. At the end of a long driveway, a woman cradled the kitten in her arms. I got out of the car. "Sorry we're late. It was farther than we thought," I said.

She nodded. Without a word, she handed the kitten to me. "OK?" she asked. I drew him close to me.

On the way home, we tried out names and settled on Kirby. As I held Kirby in my lap, I began to inspect him. His ears were filled with black gunk; fleas scurried all over his body. *What have I done?*

Within hours, we were at the animal hospital where the vet cleaned Kirby's ears. "He's one lucky cat," the vet said. "He'll be fine. And he'll probably be hearing for the first time in his life."

In a few days Kirby was a fur ball of joy, scampering around the house, climbing the curtains, and falling asleep in his favorite spot on Solomon's top bunk.

*Sabra Ciancanelli*

**Dear God, please lead me and others to Your creatures that need care.**

# Moody Rudy

**But there is a friend who sticks closer than a brother.**
—PROVERBS 18:24 (NKJV)

I could feel a tapping on my feet as I sat at my desk. Then a bite at my ankle. Our cat Rudy would not leave me alone! He had also developed a new sound—a mournful and annoying chirping that I had never heard before. As soon as I tried to lift him, he became a deadweight lowrider.

Then when I got him on the desk, he positioned himself directly in front of my computer screen, blocking my work. *How did he come up with this new routine?*

I had been battling the flu all week. I would have preferred to be in bed sleeping, but as a freelancer, I knew deadlines were deadlines. I usually enjoyed various games with "my fur boy" during my workday, but this week, drained from the flu, what I wanted was peace, not a cute cat. The chirping: that's what got my goat! It was nonstop. Now I was not only irritated but also worried about Rudy. Was *he* sick?

When I lifted him off my desk, I got down on the floor with him and lay down on my side. As I was fighting the urge to just close my eyes, Rudy put his face up to my nose and put his paw on my face. I connected with something deep in his eyes. He was simply desperate for me to feel better. It is a mystery how the Lord communicates with cats, but this feline instinctively knew something was wrong with me. Rudy's instinctual sensitivity transformed my irritation into a new appreciation for him.

As I petted Rudy and hugged him, I began to hear a soft purring response.

And I felt better myself.

*Terry Clifton*

***Thank You for the four-legged friend in my life who shows me when I need to slow down.***

# Hanging On

***All the treasures of wisdom and
knowledge are hidden in Him.***

—COLOSSIANS 2:3 (HCSB)

Years ago our family had a kitten who loved to sit in the bathroom window and look out at the backyard. Jasmine quickly learned to hop up on the toilet, jump up and grab the lower part of the window frame, then pull herself the rest of the way up and lie against the screen. Unfortunately, the window didn't have a sill, and one day she made the mistake of not looking first to see if the window was raised.

After Jasmine grabbed the window frame, she saw that she had no place to go. The scrawny little kitten hung on with all her might, meowing pitifully. Hearing her cries, I rushed into the bathroom. After one glance at her little face, I quickly raised the window and gave her rear end a boost up.

I started laughing at how Jasmine had looked, but stopped abruptly. *How often do I look that way?* I wondered. So often I rush into my own little schemes, ignoring the privilege of going to the Source of all

**164**

wisdom to ask for guidance first. Then I cry out to Him in the middle of the mess I've made, when I'm barely hanging on by my own strength. In spite of my foolishness, my Savior's loving hands are always there, ready to lift me up.

During Jesus's ministry on earth, He often amazed the people and the Jewish leaders with His teaching. They knew He hadn't been formally trained as a rabbi, yet His deep knowledge and understanding of Scripture were evident. As a believer, I can draw upon that wisdom through prayer and Bible study. Just as my cat learned to check and make sure the window was raised before jumping up, my goal is to always ask Jesus for wisdom before I act.

*Dianne Neal Matthews*

*God, am I jumping without looking again?
Please guide me in the right way to go.*

# Bitter Medicine

*We know that in all things God works
for the good of those who love him, who
have been called according to his purpose.*
—ROMANS 8:28 (NIV)

My senior cat, Julie, is usually sweet natured. But her system occasionally succumbs to a recurring illness that requires antibiotics. My husband, David, holds her as I fill a syringe with medicine. Then the adventure begins. Seven pounds of aging feline transforms into a writhing, clawing mass of viciousness. We brace ourselves, keeping our eyes and hands protected. At last, we squirt the liquid into her mouth and she swallows. Sighing, we set her down. Our job is done, and the terror is over for another day.

As Julie's health improves daily, so does her attitude. When the cycle is over, she seems grateful.

Sometimes I need to swallow "bitter medicine" in my life to grow stronger faith. Bills, illness, or whatever unpleasant circumstances—I don't always accept them peacefully. I fight, kicking and screaming. Often, my fussing causes the trial to last longer or at least make it seem longer. When it's over, I've gained nothing from my rebellion.

I'm learning to accept life's tribulations with the quiet grace and obedience that Jesus wants me to display. I'm discovering a patience within as I acknowledge the reasons behind each situation and see their necessity for my soul's refinement. As I catch glimpses of the beauty of all things working together through Him and for Him, I'm filled with wonder. And I'm thankful. I am a witness to Jesus's movement in my life as He rescues me and reassures me. And I am healed.

*Heidi Gaul*

***Taking my medicine is never fun, but with Your help I know it will make me stronger.***

# Love Stored Up

***I will bring healing to you and cure you.***
—JEREMIAH 30:17 (JPS)

There is a bench in the master bathroom next to the tub. It provides a clear view of my husband's side of the bed, and since Keith had to sleep sitting up in order to breathe, an occupant of the bench could see him clearly. On the morning before my husband died, our cat L.E. had curled onto the bench, her green eyes fixed on him. For more than thirty hours, she never moved from that spot.

The year before, when Keith had had to spend several days in the hospital, L.E. was frantic, wandering from room to room looking for him, meowing forlornly. She had always loved him and missed him deeply even when he left for a short period of time. I expected that after he died she would be as stricken as I was. But once the men from the funeral home took Keith's body from the house, L.E. left the bench and came into the kitchen to eat. I knew that she understood he wasn't coming back.

Two months after Keith died, L.E. came to me to be petted for the first time and then vanished under the bed for several days, except for meals and the litter box.

The next time she came to me, she stayed longer and vanished for a shorter time. When Keith had been gone for six months, L.E. climbed onto my lap, tucked her head under my chin, and purred. I began to think she had stored up the love Keith had given her and now was sharing it with me.

*Rhoda Blecker*

***I am grateful to You, Lord, for all the ways You have brought love into my life and all the ways You find to remind me of the love that's still there.***

# A Big Lap

***And God raised us up with Christ and seated us with him in the heavenly realms in Christ Jesus.***

—EPHESIANS 2:6 (NIV)

**M**y huge female cat, Pokey, loves to sit in my lap while I watch TV. She curls her extra-large body with practiced precision. Rarely is there more than a stray foot hanging off my lap, until Dr. Phibes shows up.

We inherited Dr. Phibes—named for a sci-fi movie character—from our son. When Ron moved from home into an apartment, he left his cat behind. Now Dr. Phibes belongs to me. Wait. I belong to him.

If Dr. Phibes decides my lap makes the perfect resting place, Pokey's presence doesn't faze him. He silently jumps on the sofa beside me and inches his front paws onto the side of my thigh. Soon his shoulders and front end have displaced half of Pokey. She glares at him. But he keeps going. Little by little, Dr. Phibes scoots farther onto my lap until he's pushed Pokey off.

I sometimes forget how big Jesus's lap is. If I hear a friend talk about the favor Jesus did for her, I'm tempted to think, *Well. You never did that for me, Lord.* Which is pretty catty.

Jesus reminds me that He has lots of room on His lap, plenty of blessings, for all of us. I don't need to whine or feel left out. I just need to climb up and ask.

*Jeanette Levellie*

***I don't know how You fit all those believers on Your lap, Lord, but I'm glad there's enough room for all of us.***

# Taking Blessings for Granted

*And my God shall supply all your need according to His riches in glory by Christ Jesus.*
—PHILIPPIANS 4:19 (NKJV)

Jersey stood still in front of the bowl I'd filled with kibble that morning. Only weeks ago, the tinkling of dry food hitting the cat's ceramic dish summoned him like a dinner bell. The scraggly white stray with black patches of fur (like Jersey cattle) had found me on my front porch enjoying a spring evening. Most likely, someone had dumped him near our rural home.

My heart couldn't resist his hungry meows, so I fed the little guy from the stash I kept for visits from my grandkitties. Which, of course, as anyone who has ever fed a stray cat knows, made me the new owner of a cat. The next morning, Jersey devoured a can of wet food. And so began his mealtime routine: gravy-covered, canned morsels in the morning, hard food for strong teeth at dinner. Until now.

Jersey looked down at the dry pieces in his bowl, then up at me. The question in his eyes was clear: *Are you serious*? *Where's the yummy wet stuff I'm supposed to get?*

How could he turn up his whiskers at a meal he once so desperately needed? Funny how quickly he forgot.

Funny how quickly I forget too. Many times I've cozied up to Jesus with my incessant cries, only to act all finicky afterward, forgetting how He blessed me. Or I complain if my need wasn't met the way I had anticipated. Honestly, what could be better than *His riches in glory* supplying my needs? So purrfectly.

*Karen Sargent*

***Thank You, Jesus, for always meeting my needs, even when I forget to be grateful.***

I have felt cats rubbing
their faces against mine
and touching my cheek with
claws carefully sheathed.
These things, to me,
are expressions of love.

JAMES HERRIOT, VETERINARIAN

# A Hard Pill to Swallow

*I have refined you, though not as silver; I have
tested you in the furnace of affliction.*

—ISAIAH 48:10 (NIV)

**M**y cat had a hacking cough; I thought it was a
hairball. Two hundred and thirty-eight dollars
later, I learned it was a respiratory infection. "You'll want
liquid antibiotics, right?" my veterinarian asked me.
"Even though they cost more."

My empty checking account leered at me. "No, I'll give
Prince a pill."

He lifted one eyebrow. "Twice a day for two weeks?
You can't miss a day."

"I can do it," I said.

But soon I switched from praying nightly for my cat to
recover to praying that I would live through the two weeks.
I put a tablet in with his food; he ate around it. I crushed
one and mixed it with liver (his favorite); he left the liver
so long it developed a crust. I wrapped a towel around
him; he clawed it to shreds and poked me with his tooth.

When I finally got the medicine down his throat, I
cried, "Yes!" and let him go—only to find the tiny white

pill lying in the corner of the room. He knocked over the TV table, he pulled down a blue curtain; I was so covered with scratches that I looked like I'd fallen on a cactus. And I was late for work again.

"You're part of a team," my manager scolded as she wrote me up—again. "I know that you're a good employee, so getting a reprimand must be a hard pill to swallow."

"What did you just say?" I asked. That's when it all clicked. I'd just received something that would make me better.

"I'll be on time from now on," I promised.

And I was.

*Linda Neukrug*

***God, is there a change I need to make that's a "hard pill to swallow"? Let me see it as an opportunity to make myself what You think I can be.***

# Healing Purrs

***Heal me, Lord, and I will be healed;
save me, and I will be saved.***

—JEREMIAH 17:14 (NIV)

A friend told me that the purring of cats has a healing power. I wasn't so sure. Perhaps it's because our cat, a large Maine coon mix that was rescued from the subway platform, is a less-than-perfect pet. Fred won't sit in my lap for more than thirty seconds and never voluntarily. He likes to wake us up at 6:00 a.m. for his breakfast, even when there's food still in the bowl. He claws at the sofa. He unloads cat hair in remarkable quantities (you could knit a sweater from the stuff we collect). Fortunately, he's good at purring.

Take out his brush, he purrs. Sit next to him on the bed, he purrs. Scratch him on the flat part of his nose, he purrs so loud I think the neighbors can hear. That his purring can be healing was revealed to me the other night.

It was 3:00 a.m., and I wasn't sleeping well. Too many things were going through my mind. I was doing my best to pray through the worries—give them back to God—without much success.

Then Fred leaped up on the bed and meowed. "No, Fred," I whispered, "it's not time for breakfast." He lay down next to my head, his tail twitching, and purred, an incredibly loud, comforting, satisfying sound.

It turned out to be just what I needed. I scratched him on the forehead and I'm not sure where the worries went, but the next time I woke up it was 6:10 a.m. Fred was letting me know he was hungry.

"Thanks for the extra ten minutes, pal," I told him. And for the purring.

*Rick Hamlin*

***God, You have so many ways of giving me Your healing touch.***

# The Sponge and the Sparrow

***She is clothed with strength and dignity;***
***she can laugh at the days to come.***
—PROVERBS 31:25 (NIV)

Here's the story of the day: A friend of mine who is ninety-six years old, born before the "first of the wars of the world," as she says, still lives in her little beach cottage, although she's been blind since the first of our wars in "Persia," as she says. "I hear pretty well, I can move around with minimal creakiness, and people are so kind to me; why would I move?"

One morning her cat captured a sparrow outside and brought it into the house in triumph. My friend heard this dramatic adventure loud and clear while washing the dishes. She barked at the cat, picked up the fluttering bird with a sponge, opened the kitchen window, tossed out the sponge and started back to washing the dishes, only to realize she was using the sparrow, who objected strenuously.

"It was all I could do not to fall down laughing," she says, "but at my age falling down is a bad idea. I got the window open again and ejected the bird, but then I laughed so hard, I think I sprained my face."

Now, this is a terrific story from every angle imaginable, it seems to me: the deft, athletic cat; the sparrow who didn't die; the sinewy old lady giggling; the smile on your face; the prayer that your smile is for my friend; and maybe best of all, the helpless laughter of the child you will just have to tell this story to sometime today.

*Brian Doyle*

***Dear Lord, for laughter and sparrows and clean dishes and kids giggling and, well, I guess, even for murderous cats, thank You most sincerely.***

# The Joy of Gratitude

*Give thanks in all circumstances; for this*
*is the will of God in Christ Jesus for you.*
—1 THESSALONIANS 5:18 (ESV)

I had never seen someone so happy to be home. My calico cat emerged from the carrier after her trip to the veterinarian and greeted my dogs as they pressed in to smell her, clearly loving every minute of their slobbering curiosity. As soon as the dogs' interest waned, Videa went to the living room and sprawled on the carpet.

Lying stretched out on her side was abnormal behavior for Videa, except when she returned home from a stressful journey. Then she would lie in the middle of the room with a look of sheer bliss in her half-closed eyes, as if soaking in the wonder of returning home.

I would have expected that, after spending the first three years of her life as a feral cat, Videa would be more cynical. I thought she might never fully enjoy her new life, thanks to learning the hard way that good things are rare and can't be trusted. But instead of letting those earlier experiences harden her heart with negativity and bitterness, she used them as reasons for gratitude.

Watching Videa relish her homecoming made me realize how much I miss in life. The hard experiences I've had make me feel I have reason to expect the worst of others and my circumstances. As a result, I often don't enjoy good things to the fullest—either because I doubt their goodness or because I'm looking for the bad things I'm sure are soon to come.

But Videa didn't let negativity spoil her opportunities for joy. She chose to be grateful instead. I suspect that is how she survived her years of feral life as well. I want to be like her, grateful in all circumstances. Then I just might have Videa's kind of joy—the joy that comes from gratitude and is God's will for me.

*Jerusha Agen*

**Lord, when doubt starts to weigh me down, lead me to choose gratitude instead.**

# Proof in the Litter Box

*He has made everything beautiful in its time.*
—ECCLESIASTES 3:11 (NIV)

Our cat, Kirby, is always getting into trouble. This time he almost killed himself swallowing a spool of thread. The emergency vet said we saved his life by bringing him in. He took X-rays and kept Kirby overnight for observation.

The next morning Kirby came home, ears-back and angry, confused and exhausted. We were told to keep him isolated, monitor the litter box, and return immediately if he was sick to his stomach.

I stayed awake all night with Kirby beside me. I watched odd movies that only seem to play in the wee hours of the morning and prayed my way to sunrise, trying not to think of a dire outcome.

The next morning Kirby went in for a follow-up visit. The vet was optimistic the thread would pass on its own. If not, Kirby would need immediate and expensive surgery.

By the fourth day, I worried the operation might need to happen. The entire afternoon, I prayed, "Please, please help him."

Right before bed, I went into Kirby's sequestered room. I combed the litter box as I'd done a hundred times. This time, the thread was there, the evidence, the source of my anxiety. I hugged Kirby and kissed him. *Phew*!

*Sabra Ciancanelli*

***Heavenly Father, the next time I get myself all stressed out, I'll remember that litter box story . . . and try to have faith in Your perfect timing.***

# A Bad Cattitude

***"The LORD make his face shine upon you
and be gracious to you; the LORD turn
his face toward you and give you peace."***

—NUMBERS 6:25-26 (NIV)

Ruffian sat in the back of a metal cage at the shelter I work at. An adult cat whose owner had passed away, he was truly beautiful, but his adopted family had found him too mean to keep. So he sat in all of his rich Himalayan glory for one month, and then another, as people cooed over his beauty but then passed him by with each angry hiss.

One day, a young woman with a sadness similar to Ruffian's walked in. She had just lost her cat to old age and was completely devastated. She was looking for a kitten, preferably a long-hair and, even though it was a long shot, a snow-pawed Himalayan. There were no kittens, but we told her there was something she might like to see and we walked her into the cat room of the shelter.

Ruffian sat back and hissed as he normally did. She opened his cage, and he howled in anger. She put her hand up to him, and he backed away with a growl. Then the miracle happened. She touched him. He stopped fighting and moved his head toward her hand for a pat. The purrs began so loudly, they sounded like a growl. This was something that could come only from a place of love.

"I'll take him. He has a broken heart just like me," she said, smiling. Then she cried as she snuggled him into her neck. We knew that something special had happened.

When loss overtakes us, sometimes anger and striking out in pain is our only response. But in praying for each other in loss, we can ask God Himself to shine His countenance upon us and to give us the peace that surpasses all understanding.

*Devon O'Day*

**God, send Your peace to the brokenhearted, and shine Your love on them.**

# A Companion in Grief

***My thoughts dwell on him still.***
—JEREMIAH 31:20 (JPS)

After my husband died, I needed his things around me. We have double sinks in the bathroom, so I left Keith's slippers neatly tucked together in front of his sink, as if he were standing there, brushing his teeth or washing his face. I wanted his hat on the hall tree by the front door, too, and his rain jacket on the chair in the kitchen. It wouldn't feel like our home without them.

The first time I came into the bathroom and found the slippers out of place, I thought I must have stumbled against them during the night. I carefully restored them to their original spot, but the next morning I discovered they'd been moved again. *OK, so I didn't stumble over them while I wasn't even here*, I thought. Nor did I think it was a message from beyond. I put the slippers back once more.

The next time I went into the bathroom, the cause became clear. L.E., our tortoiseshell cat, who had made Keith her preferred person and stayed away from me after he died, was snuggling next to the slippers, her shoulder pushed into the side of one and her head resting on top of it. She was purring as she had used to when she lay pressed against Keith on the couch.

I understood that even though L.E. now came to me for petting and slept beside me, she still remembered and missed Keith as much as I did. The slippers were not just my way of staying connected to Keith; they were hers as well.

*Rhoda Blecker*

**Lord, when I feel like I'm grieving alone, remind me that there are others who understand too.**

# Taking Time to Listen

***Thy will be done.***
—MATTHEW 6:10 (KJV)

I've never met a cat who loved to be brushed as much as eighteen-pound Prince does . . . when he's in the mood. He can stand, heavy on my lap, for up to fifteen long minutes while I brush his fur. If I seem to slow down, he gives me a sharp tap with his paw to remind me to pick up the pace.

I find the activity relaxing, so one evening, tense from a day of dropping off job applications with no results, I thought, *Why don't I brush Prince now?* So I picked up the brush and Prince. He purred for all of about thirty seconds and then jumped off my lap and ran away, as if to say, "That's quite enough of that!"

That's a lot like the way I've been with God. When I'm job hunting, I pray, "God, please find me a job today!" I want Him to listen to me and magically throw one at my doorstep. But when God seems to have something to say to me, such as, *Maybe it's time to update your résumé* or *Perhaps See's Candy Shop*—with its sign in the window saying, "Yes, if you work here, you *can* eat all the candy you want!"—*is not the best place for you to work at this time,* I jump off His lap.

All cat owners know that we have to deal with cats on their terms, not ours. But as a friend of mine said when I told her exactly what kind of job I wanted God to find for me, "Sounds like you're willing to serve God, but only as an adviser! Why don't you *listen* to God more than *instruct* Him?"

That was good advice. I've taken it, combining some prayer time with the time I spend brushing Prince.

*Linda Neukrug*

***God, when You want to speak to me, let me listen. And when I want to speak to You, let me listen too.***

# No Time for Snuggles

*"I will refresh the weary and satisfy the faint."*
—JEREMIAH 31:25 (NIV)

Our calico cat Thelma and our thirteen-year-old black Lab Cooper faithfully attend our porch parties. Cooper never leaves my husband Rick's side. Cooper lies beside his feet, happy to be included. But Thelma keeps a tight schedule. Somehow she manages to squeeze in porch parties despite her busy ways. Always in a hurry, she arrives late. She has so much to do, such a long list. Like me, I guess.

One morning, Thelma was wired. She didn't stop for a second. Usually she'd rub against our legs, but she had no time for play that day. She zipped across the porch, chasing a lizard; Rick helped it escape. Then she balanced on her hind legs on the railing and stretched up to paw at a hanging basket. The basket began to sway, and a few dried fern leaves fell from it. "No, Thelma!" I said. "Stop it!" Momentarily satisfied, she hunted the crispy fern sprigs as though they were prey.

"Thelma, rest a minute," I said. "Like Cooper. See? He never leaves us." Hearing his name, Cooper wagged his tail.

"Wonder what that cat's thinking," Rick said.

"No telling. Come here, kitty." Ignoring me, Thelma leaped off the porch and landed in the gardenia bush. "She runs from one emergency to the next," I said.

"They're emergencies of her own making," Rick observed.

That's when it hit me: I'd allowed busyness to crowd my days. Unimportant duties had distracted me from spending time snuggling beside the ones I love.

*Julie Garmon*

***Lord, I've been so busy chasing silly things.
This feels better—resting by Your side.***

# Another Year Young

*"Zacchaeus, make haste and come down,*
*for today I must stay at your house."*
—LUKE 19:5 (NKJV)

About five years ago, my niece Karin had to find a new home for her tabby cat. I hadn't particularly wanted a pet, but I opened my door. One sunny afternoon, five-year-old Kitty arrived. On distinctive blue stationery, Karin had handwritten some care tips and detailed some of Kitty's personality quirks. I thanked Karin for her comments, noted the attached veterinarian's report and set aside the papers.

My friend Jane remembers asking me how I felt about my new companion. She says I smiled big and replied, "Head over heels." The years have slipped by, and now I can hardly imagine life without Kitty. I occasionally looked for Karin's papers, but they never surfaced—until yesterday.

Sorting through an untidy stack that I've cleaned around for way too long, I spotted the unmistakable stationery. I scanned Karin's characterization of Kitty. No surprises there. But a relatively insignificant fact distressed me. Kitty is a year older than I thought. My mind raced ahead, imagining a closer-than-anticipated heartbreak: the day she's called to take her place on the graph that measures feline life expectancy.

All day long, when I saw Kitty, I felt sad. When she bumped me, I felt blue. Then last evening, she sat at the top of the staircase. I walked by and, as if to tease me, she ran down the stairs. Her burst of energy jolted me out of my anticipatory grief. Impulsively, I laughed and challenged her to a race. In the kitchen, I picked her up and thanked God for the joy of the *present* presence.

*Evelyn Bence*

***Lord, help me to appreciate the delights of today rather than anticipate the griefs of tomorrow.***

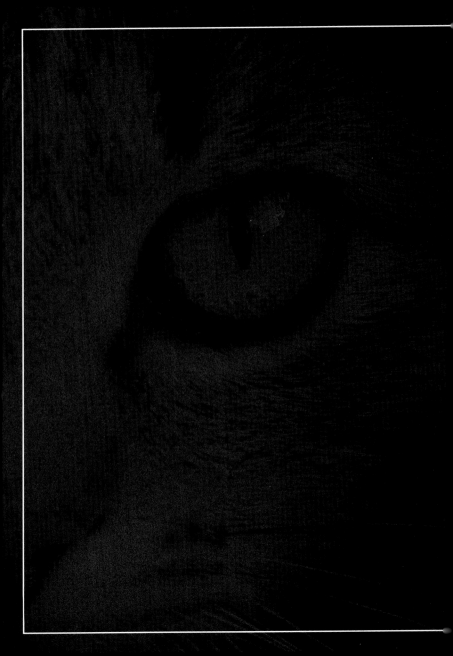

To err is human
To purr feline.

ROBERT BYRNE, AUTHOR

# A Good Day

***LORD, in the morning you hear my voice.
In the morning I lay it all out
before you. Then I wait expectantly.***

—PSALM 5:3 (CEB)

The water was boiling. I poured the five-minute Irish oatmeal into the pot and stirred, lowering the heat. Now what? I didn't usually make oatmeal for myself, and I was worried I'd end up with a stick mess clinging to the side of the pot.

*Meow,* Fred said at my feet. He gazed up toward the top of the refrigerator where we keep his brush.

"Fred," I said, "I'm trying to figure out how to cook this oatmeal."

*Meeeeooooow.* Oatmeal or not, he wanted to be brushed. I grabbed the Zoom Groom and knelt down beside him.

"You're going to have to cooperate, Fred. Paws down." He stretched out, turning into a gray-and-white puddle on the floor. I ran the brush through his thick fur. Clumps rose off his lush coat, floating like fog and then dropping to the ground or getting stuck on my sweats.

I got up and stirred the oatmeal and then returned to Fred. He began purring. *As long as I can't do anything else, I might as well pray*, I thought.

"Thank You, God, for a demanding cat, a bubbling breakfast, the snow that's melting, the run I made on just-plowed streets." Fred swiped a lazy paw at me, his signal that he was done. It wasn't very gracious, but that's his way. He'd already purred—that was my thank-you.

The clock on the stove said five minutes had passed. The oatmeal was ready, not stuck to the pot at all. Fred wandered off, his needs met for the time being. I poured my breakfast into a bowl, added some maple syrup and milk, and sat down to eat. It was going to be a good day.

*Rick Hamlin*

***I'll wait with You and for You, Lord,
whenever I have cause to wait.***

# I Won't Forget You

*"I would not forget you! See, I have written your name on the palms of my hands."*

—ISAIAH 49:15-16 (NLT)

I sighed as I fluffed the down comforter around me. My family had been with me a few days, but now they'd gone home and the house seemed hollow. I whispered to God, "I feel so alone." Rolling over, I fell asleep.

Two hours later, the icy wind howled. I sat straight up in bed and gasped. *Oh no, I forgot to put out the heated water dish for Kitty!* The temperatures had been below zero, and if she didn't have anything to drink, she might get frostbite or even freeze to death. Kitty was a feral tortoiseshell cat who preferred to be wild and fend for herself.

Quickly I bundled up, donned a wool cap with my headlamp, and pulled on mittens. I hustled out to the barn, carrying a dish filled with water to tide her over until morning.

I swung the wooden door open and heard Kitty scamper across the stack of hay. She shivered as she lapped and lapped. I pulled off my mittens and touched her. Her body felt cold to the bone. I curled up on the hay

**200**

and, although the temperature was twenty below zero, I unzipped my jacket and gently guided her next to my body. She didn't mind as I tucked my jacket around her and cooed. "I'm sorry I forgot you."

As Kitty leaned against my body, I felt the warmth of God's love and heard, *But I haven't forgotten you. I've been with you all along.* In my mind's eye, I saw God's huge hands cupped around me.

*Rebecca Ondov*

***Lord, thank You for showing me how much You love me. Amen.***

# Free as a Bird

***He rescued me from my powerful enemy,***
***from my foes, who were too strong for me.***
—PSALM 18:17 (NIV)

My cat, Ivy, adopted from a farm, proves that although you can take a cat out of the country, you can't take the country out of the cat. She loves to hunt and is an excellent mouser.

One bright spring morning, she stood before me in the living room, her stance proud. And then she dropped a surprise offering at my feet. She'd brought in a bird—an unhurt but terrified bird.

It immediately flapped its wings and flitted to a windowsill. My husband and I formulated a plan on how to catch it. Minutes later, we carried the frightened creature to our front yard, careful to lock Ivy indoors. As we set the tiny bird on our porch railing, she stood stock-still, then seemed to shake the situation off. A moment later, she flew to our maple tree, where she perched and stared at us as if to say thank you. As we watched, she took flight and was gone.

Years ago, Jesus rescued me from the dangerous and damaging life choices I'd made. While I was frightened and confused, He picked me up and held me in the palm of His hand. He carried me away from the hurt and the pain and led me to a place of safety. I no longer need to hide my face in shame or act in fear.

Today I rest in the security of His grace and fly unrestrained, covered in the limitless grace He provides. I am free, indeed. Free as a bird.

*Heidi Gaul*

***God, as I watch the birds today, I thank You for the genuine freedom I've experienced in You.***

# Bobby's Bark

*"They think that they will be heard for their many words."*
—MATTHEW 6:7 (RSV)

There was no point in my even trying out for the open spot in dance class, I wailed to my mother. "Gracie says her dad is friends with the man who owns the school. She says her mother was a famous dancer. She says—"

"Gracie says, Gracie says," Mother interrupted my lament. "You know what this reminds me of? Bobby's bark."

Bobby was our little black cocker spaniel who yap-yapped to the world that he owned our yard. We had one other pet—a black-and-white cat named Domino, who liked to sleep on the front steps in the sun.

Three doors down the street lived a Doberman pinscher, five times Bobby's size and who occasionally came strolling past. Rounding the corner on his patrol, Bobby would stop short. Ferocious bark strangling in his throat, he'd streak for the house, bound up the steps, and stand behind Domino.

The Doberman, hunting instinct triggered, would veer onto the yard. Whereupon Domino stood up, huge and terrible, no longer the gentle pet that spent nights on my

**204**

bed. Back arched, fur bristling, dagger teeth exposed, he'd emit a fearsome hiss.

At this point in the familiar drama, the Doberman appeared to recollect an errand farther up the street. Long legs sidestepping daintily, he'd continue his afternoon ramble. Domino would sit down and wash. And Bobby, when the bigger dog was out of sight, would resume his rounds, barking as loudly as ever.

In fact, neither Gracie nor I got into dance school that year. But I'd learned a priceless distinction between noise and substance.

*Elizabeth Sherrill*

***Let all my words today, Father, match the reality they represent.***

# Sunshine Learns to Purr

***Hatred starts fights, but love pulls a quilt
over the bickering.***

−PROVERBS 10:12 (MSG)

One day my son Jeremy brought me a five-week-old orange kitten he'd found screaming in the woods, high in a tree. She was tiny, beautiful, helpless, and hungry. I carried her around like a baby—even rocked and sang, "You are my sunshine." Which then inspired her name: Sunshine.

She grew into a giant creature—a super cat from another planet, with keen wisdom and a will of iron. She bit and scratched me daily. I scolded her loudly, "No! Bad!" Undaunted, she stood on her mighty hind legs like a boxer, punching and scratching me. She roamed our house like a wild beast of prey, hiding in obscure places to jump out, startling my husband, me, and my two indoor cats. Sometimes when I tried to rock her, she glared at me with wide amber eyes, then stuck out a giant orange paw and slapped my face.

I called my aunt Lillian, a fellow cat rescuer, and she told me, "Mannie, you don't know what she had to go through to survive or what her mama taught her. She has feral genes. Poor little thing."

That very day, I whispered to Sunshine, "I love you. Always will." I kissed her face several times. She seemed to like my face on hers. So we butted heads often. Softly. Sometimes she initiated it, her eyes closed. Her scratching and biting didn't suddenly stop. But she relaxed and even snoozed on the back of my husband's chair, while he bravely read.

Now she sleeps with us nightly, waiting patiently for me to tuck her in underneath the soft blanket.

She's learned to purr.

*Marion Bond West*

***Oh, Father, teach me how to love unlovable people, who've most likely been hurt.***

# My Cat

***My Lord God will wipe away the tears from all faces.***
—ISAIAH 25:8 (JPS)

The day I walked into the bathroom and found my cat L.E. on the rug in front of my sink, rather than the rug in front of my late husband Keith's sink, I realized she had finally become my cat.

For three years after Keith died, I thought it was a lost cause. I knew she was grieving Keith from the first, and since I, too, was grieving, I hoped we could comfort each other, but she stubbornly refused to acknowledge it as a companionship of loss. She clung to her memories—lying pressed against his slippers in the bathroom or sleeping on his side of the bench at the bottom of our bed—without seeming to understand I would cuddle and pet her just as I petted Anjin, the greyhound.

L.E. always seemed far more aloof with me than she had ever been with Keith. She never meowed at me, never curled up in my lap on the sofa. I felt she wanted me to leave her alone, so I did. I had to be patient. Every so often, I tried to play with her, but she just walked away, tail in the air.

In the beginning of the fourth year, Anjin had to have her teeth cleaned, and that involved my taking her to the vet early in the morning and returning home without her. The house seemed so empty. My dog's comforting presence as he followed me around or pressed up against my side was not there, and I missed it. The emptiness reminded me of missing Keith.

For the first time in a long while, I cried and hugged L.E. because I really needed her. Later that afternoon, she moved to my side of the bathroom. Even after I brought Anjin home, L.E. stayed by my side.

*Rhoda Blecker*

***Thank You for reminding me that reaching out,
to You and to others, can bring rewards.***

# Kirby Loves Henry

*People can tame all kinds of animals,*
*birds, reptiles, and fish.*
—JAMES 3:7 (NLT)

I'm usually upstairs working when I hear the shriek of our dog, followed by a howl and the growl of a very angry cat. Sounds that can mean only one thing: Kirby attacked Soda again.

Our cat Kirby is an alpha male. All white and strong but for a low belly that is getting increasingly plump, he is an odd sort of bully. He hides under the skirt of the living room chair and waits for his victim, and then when the moment is right he pounces. A few times, he jumped right on Soda's back and rode him like a pony until Soda shook him off.

We've tried all the pet suggestions of how to make Kirby accept our dog. Most of the time, they get along fine. It's just that every once in a while something happens and a cat-and-dog fight ensues.

Kirby's saving grace is that he loves to sleep with our son Henry. Every night, just as Henry gets into bed, Kirby follows. He jumps up and settles right at Henry's feet.

Last night, Henry spent the night at a friend's house. I went to bed early and when I woke in the morning and came downstairs, I noticed Kirby was curled up on the hardwood floor right at the foot of the front door.

"He slept there all night," my husband, Tony, said, "He misses Henry."

And so it is—a beautiful gesture of love from an unlikely source.

*Sabra Ciancanelli*

**Dear Lord, thank You for cats and dogs that keep life interesting. Bless our family and help make us complete.**

# Prescription for Laughter

***Continue earnestly in prayer, being vigilant
in it with thanksgiving.***

—COLOSSIANS 4:2 (NKJV)

I was worried. My cat Prince was terribly sick. I felt like a meanie dragging him to the vet but prayed for the strength to get Prince into his carrier without my needing a doctor, too, for bites and scratches.

I accomplished my goal, and the vet said Prince sounded and looked a lot worse than he was. She called in a prescription anyway that would speed his recovery.

Still I worried. *God, she only examined Prince for a few minutes. I've been hearing his hacking cough for days. Please make sure he is all right.* My worry was in overdrive and gave me a headache, but before I could buy aspirin, I needed to settle Prince back at home.

Finally, I headed over to pick up his prescription. The pharmacist checked the shelf and said, "There is nothing here, Linda." I was annoyed. My vet was usually super-reliable, which was why I'd chosen her.

I turned to go, then had a thought. "By any chance, is there a prescription for Prince Neukrug?" And, of course,

212

there was. I explained to the pharmacist that Prince could not come in to pick up his prescription, so he sent his courier.

Both of us had a good laugh, and when I left the store—without aspirin—my headache was gone.

*Linda Neukrug*

***Laughter is good medicine, Lord. Thank You for letting me find it in the middle of worrying.***

# Bringin' a Friend Home for Dinner

*"Here I am! I stand at the door and knock. If anyone hears my voice and opens the door, I will come in and eat with that person, and they with me."*

—REVELATION 3:20 (NIV)

Little Gray was the cat next door. From the time he was a kitten, he would show up at the door, meowing loudly for food he preferred over that which he got at home. As Little Gray grew, he brought more and more friends for supper. Some of Little Gray's friends decided to stay, while others only stopped by for a meal, but they were all welcomed.

One night Little Gray even brought a possum, who ate right alongside the cats gathered at the many bowls I laid out nightly. Twenty pounds of food a week and this nightly ritual at suppertime remind me of the table that God sets for all of us. There is always room at the table of the banquet of love, and the feeling of welcome surpasses anything else in comparison.

What spoke to me most about Little Gray, though, was his willingness to invite another to the table. He was never selfish, never trying to keep the banquet all to himself. And he wasn't ashamed to offer a seat at the table for fear of another's opinion. Instead, he shared the bounty with others, and there was always more than enough.

Little Gray just opened the door to those who showed up, and there was fellowship at the table. We, too, are offered opportunities every day to share the bounty of God's table with those in our circles. But sometimes we fail to open the door to others, maybe because we are afraid of how we will be perceived, or maybe because we think there will not be enough to go around.

But at God's table, there is always more than enough love to share. In fact, the amount of love at the table grows every time we open the door and let others in.

*Devon O'Day*

***God, please break down my fear of sharing Your bounty of love with a needy world. Amen.***

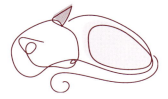

# His Quiet Place

*"Come with me by yourselves to a quiet place and get some rest."*

—MARK 6:31 (NIV)

Tommy is my long-haired marmalade cat. He just showed up one day years ago and elected to stay. I was determined not to feed him, lest we end up with yet another cat. But after a month of his curling around my feet and sleeping on the porch, I realized the decision wasn't mine.

I don't know this little fellow's history, but I've learned he doesn't like being indoors and he loathes being carried and only tolerates our other pets. He is, indeed, a cat unto himself.

Today, as I headed for the mailbox, Tommy appeared. He raced up the stairs to meet me, meowing. I couldn't resist him. I never can. He hopped up almost before I'd settled into the rocker. As he purred, I stared into his green-gold eyes, fascinated.

*Why did Jesus drop this cat onto my lap—my life?*

I take a deep breath. Tension slips free from my shoulders and neck. I scratch this orange ball of fluff under his chin, and he rolls onto his back. He looks ridiculous, all four chunky paws pointing skyward. I hear gentle laughter and realize it's mine.

Minutes pass, and Tommy decides he's had enough. He jumps to the floor and scurries out of sight. I close my eyes. The breeze is soft on my face, and the deep resonance of our wind chimes stills my thoughts. I rock more slowly.

This ten-pound cat—the one Jesus picked—has led me to this quiet place. Jesus is resting with me. This is peace.

*Heidi Gaul*

*Thank You, Jesus, for quiet places and beautiful felines and Your perfect peace.*

# Acknowledgments

Every attempt has been made to credit the sources of copyrighted material used in this book. If any such acknowledgment has been inadvertently omitted or miscredited, receipt of such information would be appreciated.

Scripture quotations marked (CEB) are taken from the *Common English Bible*. Copyright © 2011 by Common English Bible.

Scripture quotations marked (ESV) are taken from *The Holy Bible, English Standard Version*. Copyright © 2001 by Crossway Bibles, a division of Good News Publishers. Used by permission. All rights reserved.

Scripture quotations marked (HCSB) are taken from the *Holman Christian Standard Bible*. Copyright © 1999, 2000, 2002, 2003, 2009 by Holman Bible Publishers, Nashville, Tennessee. All rights reserved.

Scripture quotations marked (JPS) are taken from *Tanakh: A New Translation of the Holy Scriptures according to the Traditional Hebrew Text*. Copyright © 1985 by the Jewish Publication Society. All rights reserved.

Scripture quotations marked (KJV) are taken from the *King James Version of the Bible*.

Scripture quotations marked (MSG) are taken from *The Message*. Copyright © 1993, 2002, 2018 by Eugene H. Peterson.

Scripture quotations marked (NCV) are taken from *The Holy Bible, New Century Version*. Copyright © 2005 by Thomas Nelson. Used by permission. All rights reserved.

Scripture quotations marked (NIV) are taken from *The Holy Bible, New International Version®, NIV®*. Copyright © 1973, 1978, 1984, 2011 by Biblica, Inc. Used by permission. All rights reserved worldwide.

Scripture quotations marked (NKJV) are taken from the *New King James Version®*. Copyright © 1982 by Thomas Nelson. Used by permission. All rights reserved.

Scripture quotations marked (NLT) are taken from the *Holy Bible, New Living Translation*. Copyright © 1996, 2004, 2007, 2015 by Tyndale House Foundation. Used by permission of Tyndale House Publishers Inc., Carol Stream, Illinois. All rights reserved.

Scripture quotations marked (RSV) are taken from the *Revised Standard Version of the Bible*. Copyright © 1946, 1952, 1971 by the Division of Christian Education of the National Council of the Churches of Christ in the United States of America. Used by permission.

# A Note from the Editors

We hope you enjoyed *Faithful Purrs*, published by Guideposts. For more than seventy-five years, Guideposts, a nonprofit organization, has been driven by a vision of a world filled with hope. We aspire to be the voice of a trusted friend, a friend who makes you feel more hopeful and connected.

By making a purchase from Guideposts, you join our community in touching millions of lives, inspiring them to believe that all things are possible through faith, hope, and prayer. Your continued support allows us to provide uplifting resources to those in need. Whether through our communities, websites, apps, or publications, we inspire our audiences, bring them together, and comfort, uplift, entertain, and guide them. Visit us at guideposts.org to learn more.

We would love to hear from you. Write us at Guideposts, P.O. Box 5815, Harlan, Iowa 51593 or call us at (800) 932-2145. Did you love *Faithful Purrs?* Leave a review for this product on guideposts.org/shop. Your feedback helps others in our community find relevant products.

*Find inspiration, find faith, find Guideposts.*
Shop our best sellers and favorites at
**guideposts.org/shop**
Or scan the QR code to go directly to our Shop.